⚘ TWENTY-ONE GREAT VOICES ⚘

POWERFUL SHAPERS OF CHRISTIANITY FROM THE
FIRST THROUGH THE TWENTIETH CENTURIES

BY JEFFREY JON RICHARDS

Wipf and Stock Publishers
Eugene, Oregon

WIPF AND STOCK PUBLISHERS
199 W 8th Avenue, Suite 3
Eugene OR 97401

http://www.wipfandstock.com

TWENTY-ONE GREAT VOICES
POWERFUL SHAPERS OF CHRISTIANITY FROM THE
FIRST THROUGH THE TWENTIETH CENTURIES

By Jeffrey Jon Richards

Copyright© 2002 by Jeffrey Jon Richards

ISBN: 1-59244-085-1

TWENTY-ONE GREAT VOICES:
POWERFUL SHAPERS OF CHRISTIANITY FROM THE FIRST THROUGH THE TWENTIETH CENTURIES

≈ CONTENTS ≈

Introduction 5

1.
Early Christianity:
The Foundation

Polycarp of Smyrna 11
Origen 15
Augustine 21
Jerome 25
Benedict 29

2.
Medieval Christianity:
The Feud

Charlemagne 35
Urban II 39
Innocent III 43
Peter Abelard 47
John Wyclif 51
Erasmus 57

3.
Reformation Christianity:
The Faction

Martin Luther	65
Ulrich Zwingli	71
Johann Heinrich Bullinger	75
William Farel	79
John Calvin	85
Theodore Beza	91
Ignatius Loyola	95

4. Late Christianity:
The Faith

John Wesley	101
George Whitefield	107
Lewis Sperry Chafer	113

Conclusion 135

Bibliography 137

❧ INTRODUCTION ❦

Though the Christian Church is entering into the third millennium, there is an incredible lack of understanding concerning its history and importance. American religious life is characterized by one word — pluralism. The three major religious divisions continue to be Catholicism, Judaism and Protestantism; however, a variety of alternative world religions and ideologies in recent years have captured the allegiance of countless numbers. For example, the Islamic faith continues to gain many faithful adherents not only in third world countries, but also in Europe and the Unites States. The New Age movement, though not specifically a religion, has been accepted by millions and is growing rapidly. Cults and sects continue to proselytize and are gaining in great numbers new disciples. Many today would have a difficult time understanding Christianity because of such factors as the acceptance on the part of many Americans of world religions such as Buddhism, Hinduism, Confucianism and Islam. Mormonism, Jehovah's Witnesses, and the Unification Church in recent years have greatly swelled their ranks with faithful followers. Even Christianity with its hundreds of denominations seems to be more divisive than unifying.

For the one who desires a better understanding of his/her Christian roots, viewing the lives of select, significant Christians from the first through the twentieth centuries will give perspective to what is occurring religiously at the beginning of the twenty-first century not only in the United States but worldwide. The lives of these twenty-one key Christians continue to have an impact. This book will allow you to gain an appreciation for the legacy of the Christian Church. The book discusses martyrs - those fearless followers of Christ who gave of their lives as an ultimate testimony of their personal faith. Some of those discussed had charges of heresy leveled against them. Augustine describes his dramatic conversion experience and how he was saved from living a wasted life. You will read about monasticism, religious wars, feuds between the Church and the monarchy, and the most massive schism in the Church, the Reformation. The life of George Whitefield is briefly examined. He was a fiery evangelist whose message of grace and salvation unified the First Great Awakening during the eighteenth century. Many today claim he is the father of the contemporary evangelical, evangelistic thrust.

I have chosen to conclude with Lewis Sperry Chafer, a Christian theologian who has greatly influenced recent controversies concerning the second coming of Christ and how the end of history will take place. Chafer had the ability to interpret the timeless truths of Scripture in a manner which captivated and inspired others. Many of Chafer's disciples are currently better known than Chafer himself. He had a direct or indirect influence upon literally hundreds of thousands of Christians worldwide.

The book gives a thread of cohesiveness throughout the centuries to enable one to gain a more comprehensive view of Christianity. In the diversity of these lives, there is unity. Each continues to speak.

Jeffrey Jon Richards
Salisbury, North Carolina
July, 2002

INTRODUCTION

TWENTY-ONE GREAT VOICES

1

Early Christianity: The Foundation

TWENTY-ONE GREAT VOICES

☙ POLYCARP OF SMYRNA ❧

Polycarp lived between 69 and 155 A.D. and is credited to have been a personal friend of the Apostle John. Tradition holds the latter was instrumental in assigning Polycarp the position of Bishop of the Church of Smyrna. Polycarp is an important figure because he was the last of the Apostolic Fathers and is considered a link between the Apostles and the Christians of the second century. He is not considered an intellectual or as gifted as some during this period, but he is extolled for his character and uncompromising attitude.

The Epistle of Saint Polycarp to the Philippians is his only work that has survived the centuries. This letter is believed to have been written near the event of St. Ignatius' death or about 107 A.D. Polycarp quoted the writings of Paul and Peter as well as the Gospels. Of particular interest is that Polycarp quotes from I Peter and the Pastoral epistles; thus, modern critics are forced to accept that Peter was the human author and that the book was not written at a later date.

Even while still a young man, Polycarp displayed his contempt for any nonapostolic teachings. He was requested to send *The Epistle of Ignatius to the Philippians* possibly in 116, and in a personal letter accompanying these epistles, one can obtain insight into the personality and characteristics peculiar to Polycarp. In this letter one can sense the apostolic characteristics that marked him. He wrote:

'Everyone who does not confess that Jesus Christ to have come in the flesh is an anti-Christ; and he who wrests the oracles of God to his own lusts and says that there is no resurrection of the body or future judgment is the first born of Satan...'[1]

Polycarp stayed in Smyrna after Ignatius was executed, He then went to Rome to consult with the Episcopate of Anicetus. There was a heated debate between the Asian and Roman churches over determining the correct time Easter should be observed. The churches in Asia Minor claimed that the resurrection should be celebrated on the day determined from the event of the Jewish Passover. They referred to themselves as "Quarto-decimans" since they observed Easter on the fourteenth day of the month of Nisan. But most churches believed Easter always came on Sunday. Polycarp discussed the matter at length with Anicetus, Bishop of Rome. Irenaeus wrote:

'And when the blessed Polycarp was at Rome in the time of Anicetus ... they immediately made peace with one another ... For neither could Anicetus persuade Polycarp not to observe what he had always observed with John the disciple of our Lord ... neither could Polycarp persuade Anicetus to observe it....'[2]

After Polycarp returned from Rome to Smyrna another major persecution of the Christians began. Instead of returning to his home, he retired into the country and spent a period of time meditating. Within a short period he was discovered and taken prisoner by those sent out by the Irenarch, the chief constable of Smyrna. Even at this traumatic time Polycarp displayed love and calmness and was allowed to pray for two hours before being escorted back to

Smyrna. When Polycarp and his captors entered the city, Herod the Irenarch and Nictes met Polycarp and made several pleas for the latter to utter the words "Lord Caesar" and thus be spared the stake. Having lost their patience at his continual refusal to give allegiance to Caesar, they finally brought Polycarp to the stadium. He was again repeatedly encouraged to swear to Caesar and denounce Christ. His reply is still considered precious by saints throughout the world. He replied, " 'Eighty and six years have I served Him and never did me wrong, how then can I blaspheme my King who has saved me?' "[3] After refusing to recant, he was tied to the stake. Because his body would not burn quickly, he was plunged through with a sword. According to witnesses the ensuing blood extinguished the fire. Polycarp's body was not allowed to be taken by the Jews since there was a prevailing fear his corpse would become an object of worship; thus, Polycarp's body was burned thoroughly. The remaining bones were collected by his followers and placed together in one location.

Polycarp is of great value historically because he is a witness to the creeds and aims of the early church. He also promoted the practicality of the daily Christian life. He is a tremendous testimony of one who could endure hardship and torture because of his profound relationship with Christ. Even though his martyrdom closed an era of persecution, his name remained immortal among Christians in the ensuing centuries. Many who would ultimately suffer martyrdom could do so bravely because of the example of Polycarp.

NOTES ON POLYCARP

1. Charles Wordsworth, *A Church History to A.D. 325* (London: Gilbert and Rivington, 1881), p. 158.

2. John Lawson, *A Theological and Historical Introduction to the Apostolic Fathers* (New York: The Macmillan Co., 1961), pp. 156-157.

3. F. J. Foakes-Jackson, *The History of the Christian Church* (New York: George H. Doran Co., 1927), p. 61.

⚜ ORIGEN ⚜

Origen greatly influenced church history because of his diverse writings. He produced copious volumes of theological works which were to have a tremendous impact upon theologians and thinkers in subsequent centuries. It has been estimated that Origen wrote six thousand volumes. Farrar says of Origen:

> 'In the history of the early church there is no name nobler or more remarkable than that of Origen. Few have rendered to the cause of Christianity such splendid services or lived from childhood to old age a life so laborious and blameless...'[1]

Origen was an Egyptian by birth and was in all probability born in Alexandria. He lived between 185 and 254 A.D. He had a very loving father who admonished his son to read Scripture; thus, Origen, while very young, memorized many passages of Scripture. His father was executed under the persecution of Septimus Servus in 202.

In 203 at the age of eighteen, he was appointed president of the Catechetical School of Alexandria. Origen was a recognized scholar even at this young age. However, he left the school after a brief period because of the impossibility of earning a livelihood by this means.

After this period his life was characterized by extreme asceticism. He renounced worldly goods and had only a minimal amount of clothes and personal possessions. He would not eat meat or drink wine and spent most of the night studying and praying. He was so determined to serve Christ that he wished not to entertain fleshly thoughts at all. In fulfillment of this desire he performed the act of castration, but he was to greatly regret this extreme act in future years since it barred him, in the opinion of many bishops, from being a clergyman. However, in 228, he was ordained a presbyter by Alexander of Jerusalem and Theoctistus of Caesarea in Palestine. Being ordained as a presbyter made the already jealous Bishop Demetrius of Alexandria outraged. The Bishop held two councils in 231 and 232. He suggested that Origen be excommunicated because of self-castration, disobeying church laws, and heresy. Perhaps, however, the primary reason was jealousy. Jerome wrote concerning Origen:

> 'Imperial Rome consents to his condemnation and even convenes a senate to censure him, not - as the rabbit hounds who now pressure him cry - not because of the novelty or heterodoxy of his doctrines but because men could not tolerate the incomparable eloquence and knowledge which made others seen dumb.'[2]

The Roman church agreed that Origen should be excommunicated, but the churches of   Palestine, Arabia, Phoenicia, and Achaia rejected it. Even during this time Origen displayed his Christlike mannerisms. Speaking about those who opposed him, Origen replied, " 'We must pity them rather than hate them; pray for them rather than curse them; for we are made for blessing, and not for cursing.' "[3]

About 250 Origen was invited to return again to Alexandria, but during the Decian persecution he was tortured terribly and cast into prison. He was so horribly treated that he lived only a short time after leaving prison.

Origen died in 254, but his prolific pen had years before determined that his thoughts would be remembered throughout history. He is considered the greatest scholar of the Ante-Nicean fathers. However, Origen cannot be considered a totally orthodox theologian. Many have referred to him as the "Schleirmacher of the Greek Church." The well-known church historian Philip Schaff wrote concerning Origen:

> 'His leaning to idealism, his predilection for Plato and his noble effort to reconcile Christianity with reason and to command it even to educated heathen and Gnostics, led him into many grand and fascinating errors.[4]

An example of his nonorthodox teachings is that of humanity's relationship with fallen spirits. Origen believed that God had created a great number of spirits. They were similar to one another. They had a nature of goodness, but it was possible for them to lose it. Origen believed that many fell from this goodness. At a particular point in the spirit's degeneration, it became a human soul and entered a baby at its birth. There were still many other material spirits.; but because they had not fallen to the same degree as those who entered man, they took other forms. He believed the stars were spirits which had not fallen as far as those of man. At death the spirit left man and the process continued. Origen maintained that Christ had a human soul. The Logos could come directly to a human body and unite with a soul. This particular spirit was not as fallen as the average spirit and had through the ages come to love the Logos; hence, the spirit was really one with the Logos. The uniting of this human soul with the Logos was not connected with the incarnation.[5]

Origen's views about the procedure the soul followed to reach God are similar to the Neo-Platonists and later mystics. His views contributed to the doctrine of purgatory. He also believed in the need of works for salvation. He wrote:

> 'The soul departing out of this world will be dealt with according to its merits, either partaking the inheritance of eternal life ... if its own works allot this to it, or committed to eternal fire and punishment, if the guilt of its evil deeds bind it over to him.'[6]

Origen did a great service in the area of exegesis. His greatest work is the *Hexapla* which is a polyglot version of the Bible consisting of the Hebrew and four Greek translations of the Old Testament. It is maintained that Ambrose encouraged Origen not only to publish his works but also to write more books. He especially encouraged him to write commentaries. Harnack wrote: " 'To the management and support of Ambrose we owe a great part of the works of Origen.' "[7]

Not only was Origen a prolific writer, but in many ways he was the first truly conscientious theologian. In ensuing christological controversies it is clearly seen that Origen could be quoted by those on opposing theological spectrums. He greatly propagated the concept of the Logos Christology, but he was also in later centuries considered heretical by many theologians. However, his Christlike character and gentleness even under persecution along with his abilities in scholarship were qualities worth emulating.

NOTES ON ORIGEN

1. Elgin Moyer, *Great Leaders of the Christian Church* (Chicago: Moody Press, 1951), p. 72.

2. Lucius Waterman, *The Post-Apostolic Age* (New York: Charles Scribner's Sons, 1901), p. 356.

3. Philip Schaff, *History of the Christian Church*, 8 vols. (Grand Rapids: William B. Eerdmans Publishing Co., 1910), 2:789.

4. Ibid., 2:791.

5. Robert Rainy, *The Ancient Catholic Church* (New York: Charles Scribner' Sons, 1902), pp. 175-177.

6. Ibid., p. 178.

7. *Geschichte der Altchristlichen Literatur*, vol. I, 328-329, quoted in F. J. Foakes-Jackson, *The History of the Christian Church* (New York: George H. Doran Co., 1927).

TWENTY-ONE GREAT VOICES

⚜ AUGUSTINE ⚜

Augustine is considered by many today to be one of the greatest theologians. His works influenced thinkers throughout the medieval period and the Reformation. Even though his theology is sometimes subjective, overall it does have a Scriptural basis.

Augustine was born at Tagaste in 354. His father was Patricius, a course and impulsive man. While his mother was a sincere Christian, she was somewhat superstitious. Since his father was not able to provide money for him to study, friends donated money, making it possible for him to study at Carthage. Studying in this Antichristian environment, he soon wandered from his mother's teachings. Manicheism was popular and promised its adherents could reach a secret wisdom. Augustine joined the sect. He began to read various philosophers, primarily the Neo-Platonists whose principles affected his thinking throughout his life. Augustine came under the influence of Ambrose and soon disassociated himself from Manicheism.[1]

Augustine began to acquaint himself with the epistles of Paul, and experienced a dramatic conversion.

> 'Thou didst call and didst cry aloud and break through my deafness. Thou didst glimmer, thou didst shine, and didst drive away my blindness ... thou didst touch me and I burned for thy peace. If I, with all that is within me, may once live in thee, then shall pain and trouble forsake me; entirely filled with

thee, all shall be life to me.'[2]

He was baptized by Ambrose at Easter in the year 387. He entered the priesthood, and most of his life was spent as Bishop of Hippo in North Africa.

Most of his treatises came from controversies with heathen and Christian heretics. The greatest controversies were with the Manicheans, who believed evil was the positive principle in the world independent of God. Augustine had controversies with the Donatists, who believed the sacraments were not effective if the priest administering them was of bad character. He also debated with Pelagians, who claimed human nature is not necessarily evil and each person has a free will to choose his own way of life. Pelagius also claimed each individual could achieve perfect righteousness and infants were born without sin. Augustine was a key factor in refuting Pelagius' doctrines.

At the center of Augustine's theology was the concept of God as complete being and all other beings only partake of being. He believed God is the only sufficient object of knowledge, but no one can completely know Him. God revealed himself to humanity by nature and Scripture. He claimed the universe was created by God in six days and creation was a voluntary act. Augustine rejected the idea of the universe being an emanation from God as seen in Neo-Platonism.

Augustine believed evil is not a positive principle but simply an absence of good. God allows evil so good can be seen more distinctly. Augustine accepted the Biblical account of Satan and his fallen angels. He believed each person is in such a horrible state, he can do nothing to save himself except by God's grace. Augustine claimed God predestinated some for salvation and others to damnation. This doctrine was to greatly affect thinkers in future centuries.[3]

Augustine had many brilliant biblical ideas but also many that were not based on Scripture. He taught salvation by the church and its sacraments. He did not believe that the church of God existed in various places and in all times. Augustine also claimed baptism is necessary for salvation. However if one was not baptized and died a martyr's death, he was christened in his own blood and saved from eternal damnation. Augustine once said: " 'Baptism is one thing, conversion of the heart is another, man's salvation is made complete through the two together.' "[4] He claimed baptism was legitimate even if a heretic or evil person administered it.

Augustine was a prolific writer, and many are familiar with his *The City of God* and *Confessions*. He wrote over 118 separate theological works. Many claim his works are today the clearest and most profound found in Latin literature. "A Spanish proverb says that every good house contains a wine cellar and every good sermon a quotation from St. Augustine."[5]

Augustine's influence upon posterity has been enormous. The primary reason for areas of agreement between Roman Catholicism and Protestantism is because of his views which are appealed to by both. He is primarily responsible for the Latin-Catholic tradition which is opposed to Greek Catholicism. Augustine, of all the church fathers, is closest to evangelical Protestantism, and many claim he is the forerunner of the Reformation because of his distinction between law and grace.[6]

NOTES ON AUGUSTINE

1. Robert Rainy, *The Ancient Catholic Church* (New York: Charles Scribner's Sons, 1902), pp. 460-461.

2. Philip Schaff, *History of the Christian Church*, 8 vols. (Grand Rapids: William B. Eerdmans Publishing Co., 1910), 3:992.

3. Frederick B. Artz, *The Mind of the Middle Ages* (New York: Alfred A. Knopf, 1953), pp. 82, 83.

4. Robert Rainy, *The Ancient Catholic Church* (New York: Charles Scribner's Sons, 1902), p. 414 quoting *De Bapt.*, vol. 4, p. 25.

5. Artz, *The Mind of the Middle Ages*, pp. 84, 85.

6. Schaff, *History of the Christian Church*, 3:1016-1018.

JEROME

Jerome is considered the most learned scholar of the Latin fathers. He continually sought after knowledge, and his life was spent writing and teaching. Even on his journey he took many books to study. His rationale was "to read the ancestors, to test everything, to hold fast the good and never to depart from the Catholic faith."[1]

Jerome was born at Striden in 346 A.D. His early life was characterized by carefreeness. However, after his baptism in 366, Jerome became a serious student. He and a friend, Bonosus, went to Gaul where Jerome ultimately spent ten years. After his return to Italy in 370, he became associated with studious men at Aquileia. After studying and debating together for three years, they parted company. Jerome and Evagrius went eastward. This trip proved to be the turning point in Jerome's life. He became deathly sick and dreamed he was standing before the judgment seat and was condemned because he was a Ciceronian instead of a Christian. After this dream he promised to end his study of classical literature.

In the autumn of 374, Jerome went to a desert in Chalis and lived there for five years. These years were periods of mental conflict. In 379 he returned to Antioch. Between 382 and 385 Jerome was in Rome.[2]

While in Rome he was urged by Pope Damascus to revise certain books of the Scripture. He prepared a revision of the Psalter and collected various Latin versions of the New Testament. Jerome started a study of the Old Testament by collating the Septuagint and versions of Aquila with the original Hebrew.[3]

In 385 Jerome went to Jerusalem with many honorable ladies following. In 386 Jerome, a friend Paula, and her daughter moved to Bethlehem. Here he built a monastery. It was during this period that he began to work on the translation of the Hebrew Bible into Latin. Realizing his deficiency in Hebrew, Jerome commenced studying the language with Bai Anina in order to translate more effectively. He also wrote may commentaries on various books of the Scriptures, revisions of the New Testament, ascetical treatises, works on place-names, and many letters. His greatest work is the Latin Vulgate which he finished about 404.[4]

Jerome's commentaries portrayed his high regard for the Scriptures. In his preface of his commentary on Isaiah he wrote: " ' He who does not know the Scripture, does not know the power of God.' "[5]

Jerome did not experience the spectacular conversion as did Paul or Augustine. Jerome wrote: " ' I was brought up on the milk of Christian faith.' "[6] Perhaps it is because of his early conversion that he wrote copious amounts of theological works.

Jerome is considered the greatest translator, textual critic and commentator of this period. There were two older Latin translations of the Bible, but they lacked quality. Jerome knew Hebrew and Greek. His greatest challenge was to take the Old Testament from Hebrew and Aramaic and translate it onto Latin. Many such as Augustine were against his work, but later his work became the authority in the Catholic church. As a commentator, he did his best work on the Old Testament. He exerted great influence on medieval exegesis. He usually limited himself to the historical context, and he was not prone to allegorize as was Origen. His commentaries had the effect of somewhat restraining the more extreme tendencies of the Alexandrian school of Biblical interpretation.[7]

Jerome also contributed to medieval historical thinking. Universal history at this point did not exist, and classical history was limited in space and time. However, after Christ this was not sufficient since Christianity was to be known universally. Eusibius of Caesarea had attempted to prepare a universal chronological chart showing the relationship of all known historical events to the incarnation. Jerome translated Eusibius' chronicle and also expanded and improved it. This gave medieval historians a beginning for scientific chronology. No library was considered complete without this work. It soon became apparent that Christians would use the date of Christ for dating history, and Jerome's chronicle made this inevitable.[8]

Today Jerome is considered orthodox even though he had ascetic tendencies. He is considered second to Augustine in scholarship. Jerome had problems in his relations with others, and he was considered to be very argumentative. However, his method of studying Scripture had a great influence on Reformation thought; thus, he is an important figure in church history.

NOTES ON JEROME

1. Philip Schaff, *History of the Christian Church*, 8 vols. (Grand Rapids: William B. Eerdmans Publishing Co., 1910), 3:968.

2. Robert Rainy, *The Ancient Catholic Church* (New York: Charles Scribner's Sons, 1902), pp. 498-499.

3. F. J. Foakes-Jackson, *The History of the Christian Church* (New York: George H. Doran Co., 1927), p. 482.

4. Ibid., p. 486.

5. Schaff, *History of the Christian Church*, 3:977.

6. Frederick B. Artz, *The Mind of the Middle Ages* (New York: Alfred A. Knopf, 1953), p. 79.

7. Norman F. Cantor, *Medieval History* (New York: The Macmillan Co., 1963), p. 91.

8. Ibid., p. 92.

⁊ BENEDICT ⁊

Benedict was born at Nursia, north of Rome, in 480. This period witnessed great intellectual and moral decadence. When he was fifteen, he left his studies primarily because he was repelled by the extreme insensitivity of his companions to the general moral decay. He sought solitude and desired to be a recluse.[1]

He lived the life of a hermit in a dark, narrow cave. Romanus, a monk, brought food for Benedict. He tied bread to the end of a long rope which also had a bell attached to it, and the sound of the bell signaled the arrival of the food. Pope Gregory once related the following story concerning Benedict:

> At one time ... the allurements of voluptuousness so strongly tempted his imagination that he was on the point of leaving his retreat in pursuit of a beautiful woman of previous acquaintance; but summoning up his courage, he took off his vestment of skins and rolled himself naked on thorns and briers, near his cave, until the impure fire of sensual passion was forever extinguished.[2]

As people heard of Benedict's fame as a godly man, many came to him. At this time Benedict was being constantly harangued by other hermits. A monastery was located nearby, and when the abbot died there, Benedict was asked to assume the position. After being at the monastery only a short period, he became disappointed primarily because the monks did not like him. There was even an attempt to poison him. Thus, Benedict returned to his cave.[3]

Benedict later sent out two disciples to find a new location for a monastery. They located a section of land between Naples and Rome on a hill near Cassino where the temple of Apollo had once stood. Upon receiving the news, Benedict took it as a sign from heaven and built a monastery there with the stones from the ancient pagan temple.[4]

At Monte Cassino, Benedict wrote a monastic constitution called the *Benedictine Rule* which is still used today. There was nothing really new in the work. Almost all of the regulations contained therein can be found in earlier rules. However, it is very concise and without a systematic order. The *Rule* is mainly concerned about the daily life of the monastery. The basis for this life is monastic virtue. The *Rule* became very important because of the force with which practical and moral direction is briefly and clearly presented. Life under the *Benedictine Rule* was one of very strict discipline and routine that did not change. However, Benedict shied away from extreme forms of asceticism. Instead of depriving and abusing the flesh, Benedict wished to preserve the health of the monks.[5]

The *Rule* commands monks to have a permanent residence in the monastery. They were required to pledge themselves to a life of total obedience to the abbot and the *Rule*. However, the abbot had to be an understanding man.

> 'Let the abbot take cognizance of the peculiarities of many; let him direct one with mild and kinds words, another with sharp reproof, but a third by attempted persuasion. Thus let

him suit himself to the peculiarity and the education of each accommodating himself to all.'[6]

The family in the monastery was not to associate with those outside; St. Benedict, therefore, chose places away from large cities such as the mountains. He desired that the monastery be independent and self-sufficient. Because of the seclusion, Benedict believed the monastery was more conducive for training.

Benedict was not a priest but was more of a missionary.

He cultivated the soil, preached to the neighboring population, directed the young monks, who in increasing numbers flocked to him and organized the monastic life upon a fixed life or rule, which he himself conscientiously observed.[7]

Benedict's greatness lay in the fact that he was a great organizer of monastic orders He was not an illustrious figure. However, he possessed great spiritual insight and is considered a primary figure in monasticism.

NOTES ON BENEDICT

1. Wilhelm Moeller, *History of the Christian Church* (London: Swan Sonnenschein and Company, 1892), p. 373.

2. Philip Schaff, *History of the Christian Church*, 8 vols. (Grand Rapids: William B. Eerdmans Publishing Co., 1910), 3:217.

3. Gustav Shchnurer, *Church and Culture in the Middle Ages*, 3 vols. trans. George J. Undreiner (Patterson, New Jersey: St. Anthony Guild Press, 1956), 1:158.

4. James Westfall Thompson and Edgar Nathaniel Johnson, *An Introduction to Medieval Europe* (New York: W. W. Norton and Company, Inc., 1937), p. 203.

5. Norman F. Cantor, *Medieval History* (New York: The Macmillan Co., 1963), p. 187.

6. Schnurer, *Church and Culture in the Middle Ages*, 1:163, quoting *The Rule of St. Benedict: A Commentary*, no page given.

7. Schaff, *History of the Christian Church*, 3:218.

2

Medieval Christianity: The Feud

TWENTY-ONE GREAT VOICES

⚜ CHARLEMAGNE ⚜

Upon the death of Pepin the Short in 768 A.D., his two sons, Carloman and Charles succeeded him and ruled jointly the Frankish kingdom. Carloman died in 771, and Charles ruled by himself.

Pope Adrian asked for Charles's assistance in engaging in battle Desiderius, the Lombard king. In 773 Charles arrived in Italy with his troops and defeated Desiderius. Thus, Charles became ruler of the Lombards. After this he routed the Saracens from the Pyrenees to the Ebro. Later he conquered the Saxons, Bohemians and the Huns.[1]

In 774 Charles went to Rome to celebrate the feast of Easter. He and Pope Adrian swore to each other their mutual allegiance. However, Charles later wanted to have sovereign rights. The question arose whether the temporal power of the Pope should be recognized. Finally in 781 they reached a compromise. The Pope gave up claims of sovereignty over Spoleta and Tuscany.[2]

In 795 Adrian died, and the next Pope, Leo III, sought to establish friendly relationships with Charles. The Pope came to depend upon Charles for protection from the hordes of heathen invaders. On Christmas day in 800, Pope Leo III placed a crown upon the head of Charles, who subsequently became known as Charles the Great, or Charlemagne. Schaff writes concerning Charlemagne:

> He stands at the head of the new Western empire, as

Constantine the Great had introduced the Eastern empire, and he is often called the new Constantine, but is as far superior to him as the Latin empire was to the Greek. He was emphatically a man of Providence.[3]

Charlemagne was an organizer. After he became emperor, he gave each tribe its own code which protected the rights of the individual. His government officials were the governors of the counties. Charlemagne also had messengers to ensure all was running smoothly throughout the kingdom. He also surrounded himself with well-educated and zealous churchmen. He sought their advice and followed it. Charlemagne was the first Germanic king since Theodoric the Ostrogoth to try to improve social conditions. Churchmen saw this and held him up as the hero of Latin Christianity instead of the Pope. However, Charlemagne did not claim to be God's prime representative on earth or try to make laws on doctrinal matters.[4]

Charlemagne was not satisfied with his position as theocratic monarch. He attempted to create an effective administration. A chancery with a staff of monastic scholars was established by Charlemagne. He also issued documents on various aspects of lay and ecclesiastical society.[5] Charlemagne depended greatly upon the clergy. He decreed that every monastery was to have a school, and he made certain that only the best scholars were teachers. The work of copying manuscripts and improving the style of handwriting was also the result of Charlemagne's endeavors. He brought about a revival in government, education, and learning for all of those under his rule.[6]

Charlemagne stressed studying the Scriptures. He exhorted the clergy to preach only what was found in Scripture and nothing else.

He asked Alcuin to prepare a new edition of Scripture. Many historians claim that Charlemagne translated the Old Testament himself into German. He also made efforts to restore penance.[7]

Charlemagne is remembered as a great religious leader as well as an outstanding political figure.

NOTES ON CHARLEMAGNE

1. E. S. Foulkes, *A Manual of Ecclesiastical History* (Oxford: John Henry Parker, 1851), p. 253.

2. Gustav Schnurer, *Church and Culture in the Middle Ages*, 3 vols. trans. George J. Undreiner (Patterson, New Jersey: St.Anthony Guild Press, 1956), 1:450-454.

3. Philip Schaff, *History of the Christian Church,* 8 vols. (Grand Rapids: William B. Eerdmans Publishing Co., 1910), 4:238.

4. Norman F. Cantor, *Medieval History* (New York: The Macmillan Co., 1963), p. 222.

5. Ibid., p. 233,

6. Frederick B. Artz, *The Mind of the Middle Ages* (New York: Alfred A. Knopf, 1953), p. 195.

7. Foulkes, *A Manual of Ecclesiastical History,* p. 256.

⁊ Urban II ⁊

Otto, who took the name Urban II, was a pupil of Bruno. Otto later entered the service of Gregory VII who made him cardinal-bishop of Ostia. Gregory VII also sent him to Germany to be the papal emissary, which was a very difficult task. He assumed the name of Urban II and was Pope from March 12, 1088, to July 29, 1099. He spent his rule primarily in various areas outside of Rome. Urban began to show great enthusiasm for the movements to the holy land.[1]

Otto, the son of the Baron of Champagne, was a tall, powerfully built man. He had much ability, a keen and penetrating mind, and great oratorical talents. A chronicler once said about him that he was "remarkable in life and character and a pattern to all."[2]

Guibert, the anti-Pope, ruled most of Rome. He detested Urban, and the latter, not feeling safe in his area of rule, went to southern Italy among the Normans. Emperor Henry was tired of the struggle with Rome, but Urban would not compromise with Henry, who had forced Gregory from St. Peter's. Urban needed someone to lead the way to conquer by force. Conrad was the man used by the church. Now it was possible for Urban to return to Rome. However, most of the clergy was giving tribute to Guibert, and the people of the country did not know who to consider as their Pope. Urban knew his position was weak, and he began to preach the need for the Crusades, which was one of the first steps in changing the leadership of Europe from the emperor to the Pope.[3]

In March 1095, Urban called a council to meet at Placentia to discuss such matters as schisms. After the Council of Placentia, Urban toured in Italy and France for the following eight months.

In November Urban held another council in Clermont. Great crowds gathered to this council. Urban's preaching and religious incentives resulted in a widespread movement of defending Christianity and taking it to others who were not of the same religion. Urban urged them to take up the cross. He used vivid pictures to paint a picture of the need to fight. When he finished speaking the assembly cried, " *'Deus vult! Deus vult!'* " (It is the will of God).[4] Men marched forward ready to fight for Christ.

Urban's appeal was built mainly around the threat of invasion by Islam and the tales of defilement of holy places. However, it is possible that Urban also realized that a crusade, if victorious, would restore prestige to the church. It was a great gamble because if it failed, it would be devastating for the church.

Urban left Clermont on December 2 and went to Limousin. In April he visited monasteries in Aquitaine. He moved through Gascony into the lands of Count Raymond, all the while preaching the cause of the cross and the need to bring the movement to others. He then moved northward to visit the monastery of Moissac. He proceeded to Toulouse to discuss plans for a crusade with Count Raymond. On July 5, Urban opened the Council at Nimes, and it was here that Raymond promised to take up the cross and join the crusade movement. The council closed on July 14, but before it ended, the brother of the king of France said he would lead the crusades. Urban left France in August. By 1096, crusades from France and Flanders marched to the ports of the Adriatic. Urban's plans for the crusades would be carried out.[5]

In 1096 the first crusade regained Jerusalem. The kingdom of Jerusalem was initiated and governed by the leaders who had won the struggle. However, Urban died two weeks after the fall of Jerusalem and did not even hear of the news of the victory. Urban is recognized as being one of the primary innovators and promoters for the initiation of the crusades.[6]

NOTES ON URBAN II

1. Philip Schaff, *History of the Christian Church*, 8 vols. (Grand Rapids: William B. Eerdmans Publishing Co., 1910), 5:70, 71.

2. George Archibald Campbell, *The Crusades* (New York: Robert M. McBride and Company, 1938), p. 32.

3. Ibid., pp. 33, 34.

4. Ibid., p. 39.

5. Kenneth M. Setton, gen. ed., *A History of the Crusades*, 5 vols. (Philadelphia: University of Pennsylvania Press, 1955), vol. 1: *The First Hundred Years*, edited by Marshall W. Baldwin.

6. B. K. Kuiper, *The Church in History* (Grand Rapids: William B. Eerdmans Publishing Co., 1964), p. 121.

⚜ **INNOCENT III** ⚜

Innocent III wielded the power of the papacy from 1198 to 1216. He was a man of personal humility and piety and had high conceptions of the papal office. Many believe that the papacy under his direction reached the greatest height she has ever obtained.

When Henry VI died, the German states were divided politically. One part supported Philip of Swabia, Henry's brother, and another group supported Otto of Brunswick. Innocent took advantage of this turmoil to gain power. He obtained Italy and present day Germany. Philip began gaining more power than Otto; thus, Innocent obtained an agreement with him that the claims should be submitted to the judgment of the court which he controlled. However, Philip was murdered in 1208, and Otto IV was again in power. Innocent acquired from Otto a guarantee of the areas of the papal states. He also obtained a promise that Otto would stop controlling German episcopal elections. Innocent crowned Otto as emperor in 1209 after the various agreements were reached. However, Otto soon forgot his promises. This stirred Innocent's anger; thus, he chose Frederick II in 1212 as the one to rule. He renewed all vows with Frederick that Otto had broken. In 1214 Otto was completely defeated by Philip II, and he abnegated his position to Frederick. Innocent had defended his papal claims, and he chose the next ruler. Everyone now realized the importance of the papacy.[1]

Innocent had no qualms about the power associated with his

position. In the first sermon he preached after he was elected, he said:

> 'For to me it is said in the Prophets, "I have this day set thee over nations and over the kingdoms, to root out and pull down and to destroy and throw down, to build and to plant." To me it is said in the book of the Apostles, "I will give unto thee the keys of the kingdom of heaven; and whatsoever thou shalt loose on earth shall be loosed in heaven." The successor of Peter is the Vicar of Christ....'[2]

Innocent had no intentions of attacking the forces that threatened the leadership of the church. Instead, by several methods he intended to extend his papal influence on western Europe and control learning, piety, and power. He wanted a new balance between the church and the secular powers. To achieve his goals, he felt he must first reconstruct the administration of the church. Innocent decided he must have control with an absolute papal monarchy in the church. In order to have this central control, he commanded that only bishops could perform confirmation and ordination of priests. Also, every member of the church was required to confess their sins to a priest and receive the Eucharist at least once a year; thus giving the priesthood authority over the laity.[3]

Innocent's greatest victory was over King John of England. An argument arose between Innocent and King John over a disputed election which was appealed to Rome. Innocent rejected the candidates in the election and chose one of his friends instead. King John refused to allow Innocent's friend to enter England; therefore, Innocent placed England under an interdict in 1208.[4] This meant there could be no church services in all of England. The King's subjects were not to obey him because he was no longer recognized king by Rome.[5] Consequently, King John seized much land from the English church. Innocent persuaded Philip Augustus to prepare to invade England. John was so frightened that he accepted Innocent's friend as archbishop, and England became the fief of the papacy.[6]

Innocent made plans to bring the Albigensian heretics back into the church by sending outstanding preachers to preach to them. When Innocent saw this was not successful, he launched a crusade against these heretics. Northern French barons also took part in hopes of obtaining more land for themselves. At the Battle of Truret, the southern forces were defeated. This opened the door for the French crown to eventually acquire the wealthy lands of Languedoc.[7]

Schaff sums up the life of Innocent in these words:

> As the spiritual sovereign of Latin Christendom, he had no rival. At the same time he was the acknowledged arbiter of the political destinies of Europe from Constantinople to Scotland. He successfully carried into execution the high-set theory of the papal theocracy and anticipated the Vatican dogmas of papal absolutism and infallibility.[8]

Thus, during the reign of Innocent III, the church rose to its greatest height of temporal power.

NOTES ON INNOCENT III

1. Williston Walker, *A History of the Christian Church* (New York: Charles Scribner's Sons, 1918), pp. 286, 287.

2. James Westfall Thompson and Edgar Nathaniel Johnson, *An Introduction to Medieval Europe* (New York: W. W. Norton and Co., Inc., 1937), p. 645 quoting *Europe and the Church Under Innocent III*, p. 15.

3. Norman F. Cantor, *Medieval History* (New York: The Macmillan Co., 1963), p. 485, 486.

4. Ibid., p. 490.

5. B. K. Kuiper, *The Church in History* (Grand Rapids: William B. Eerdmans Publishing Co., 1964), p. 125.

6. Cantor, *Medieval History*, p. 491.

7. Ibid., pp. 491, 492.

8. Philip Schaff, *History of the Christian Church*, 8 vols. (Grand Rapids: William B. Eerdmans Publishing Co., 1910), 5:152.

MEDIEVAL CHRISTIANITY: THE FEUD

⁓ PETER ABELARD ⁓

The most famous scholar of the twelfth century was born near Nantes in 1079. At an early age Peter Abelard manifested an unusual love for knowledge. His father had been in the military and had groomed young Peter for such a position, but he gladly relinquished it to a younger brother. We read in one of his autobiographical letters:

> '...that I might be educated in the lap of Minerva. And inasmuch as I preferred the equipment of dialectic to all the teachings of philosophy, I exchanged those weapons for these, and to the trophies of war preferred the conflicts of discussion. Thereafter, perambulating divers provinces in search of discussion, wherever I had heard the study of this art to flourish, I became an emulator of the Peripatetics.'[1]

Abelard went to Paris and studied with William of Champeaux. Abelard challenged him on the subject of universals, and finally William had to agree he was wrong. Abelard opened a school, and many came to listen to him. However, he had greatly angered many of the authorities, and they drove him from one place to another. Next Abelard decided to study under the renowned doctor, Anselm of Laon. In a style characteristic of Abelard, he harangued this known scholar as only short of stupid. He said of Anselm, " ' When he lighted a fire, he filled his house with smoke instead of lighting it with the blaze.' "[2]

One sees quite clearly that Abelard was a vain man who loved to argue. He soon found himself in trouble with the church mainly because of the manner in which he stated his views rather than his actual beliefs. He taught that the difference between paganism and the Gospel was not as great as that between the Old and New Testaments. He endeavored to show how the church fathers were not in agreement with one another. Abelard wrote that there were 158 theological problems with the church fathers' theological views. And of course these accusations greatly disturbed many of his contemporaries. He also pointed out that many of the earlier works portrayed poor logic, but Abelard was overbalanced in the use of reason.[3]

Abelard's concept of the Trinity brought charges of modalism and Arianism. The Trinity, he claimed, was related to God's absolute perfection. He divided God into spheres of power, wisdom and love - which he respectively ascribed to the Father, Holy Spirit and Son. Many severe charges were brought against Abelard because of this view.[4]

His primary doctrine, which he called Conceptualism, was a blending of Realism and Nominalism. It was Abelard's Conceptualism that was the basis of thought for the philosophers of the thirteenth century, primarily Magnus and Aquinas. Abelard was the opposite of a religious mystic. St. Bernard characterized Abelard as

> '....trying to make void the merit of the Christian faith when he deems himself able by human reason to comprehend God altogether. The man is great in his own eyes. He sees nothing as an enigma ... but looks on everything face to face.'[5]

MEDIEVAL CHRISTIANITY: THE FEUD

At the apex of Abelard's fame he met Heloise, and very quickly a love affair commenced. Heloise was the niece of Fulbert, canon of Notre Dame, and he detested Abelard. The exposed love affair led to Abelard's demise in ecclesiastical circles, and also many of his peers no longer showed him their respect. Since he was condemned by the church, many of the young scholars looked upon him as a man to be admired. From all over Europe they came to listen to his brilliant disputations. Many of the conservatives watched with fear as Abelard became more popular. Soon those who were jealous of him brought charges of heresy against him. In 1140 Abelard demanded that those who were accusing him should meet before a council at Sens. Bernard was the primary leader of the opposition against Abelard. Everyone was excited about the expected debate between Abelard and Bernard. The two were opposites. Abelard was loose morally and a philosopher while Bernard was the example of holiness, and he had taught popes. However, Abelard decided not to debate St. Bernard for some unknown reason. Instead of a long dramatic speech, he merely muttered, "I appeal to Rome," and walked out of the hall.[6] Because of this instance, Abelard lost much of his popularity. He went to Cluny, and Peter the Venerable received Abelard as an esteemed guest. There he spent the last two years of his life.

Peter Abelard died on April 21, 1142, and his body was taken to the Paraclete. The motto over his tomb read:

'The Socrates of the Gauls, the great Plato of the Occidentals, our Aristotle, who was greater or equal to him among the Logicians! Abelard was the prince of the world's scholars ... conquering all things by mental force....'[7]

NOTES ON PETER ABELARD

1. Carl Stephenson, *Mediaeval History* (New York: Harper and Brothers, 1935), p. 421 quoting *The Letters of Abelard and Heloise*, no page given.

2. Ibid., p. 421.

3. Frederick B. Artz, *The Mind of the Middle Ages* (New York: Alfred A. Knopf, 1953), p. 257.

4. Philip Schaff, *History of the Christian Church*, 8 vols. (Grand Rapids: William B. Eerdmans Publishing Co., 1910), 5:624, 625.

5. Artz, *The Mind of the Middle Ages*, pp. 258, 259.

6. George Archibald Campbell, *The Crusades* (New York: Robert M. McBride and Company, 1938), pp. 203, 204.

7. Schaff, *History of the Christian Church,* 5:620.

JOHN WYCLIF

John Wyclif is called the "morning star of the Reformation." He is believed to have been born in 1324 in Yorkshire. At times he was an embittered and unhappy person who manifested neurotic tendencies. Many claim that Wyclif was a Platonist.[1]

Historians record that John Wyclif was not an original thinker. Thompson claims that he was great for the following reason:

> The combination of his ideas, ceaselessly and forcefully put forward in both Latin and English, makes him as thoroughgoing a radical as the conservative Protestant leaders of the sixteenth century. There is little that separates him from them except time.[2]

He was philosophically akin to Thomas Aquinas since they both felt that faith and reason could coexist. However, Aquinas was humanistic since he appealed to Aristotle, whereas Wyclif sought reconciliation between faith and reason from a literal interpretation of the Scriptures. The writings of St. Augustine also greatly influenced Wyclif. His love for the Scriptures made him strive to make them available beyond academic circles. The translation of the Bible into English was not performed by Wyclif himself, but he is given credit for supervising the translation into English.[3]

By 1360, Wyclif had become well-known at Oxford. Not only was

Wyclif a professor, but he was also an ordained priest and held a parish in the country. His favor at court benefited him when Pope Gregory XI condemned as heresy eighteen of Wyclif's opinions. He still kept his position at the university. However, as he became known as a rebel against the church's authority, many at Oxford no longer supported him.[4]

In 1374 after he returned from a trip in France, Wylcif began to speak as a reformer at Oxford and London against the Pope and his secular power. In one of his tracts, he claimed that the bishop of Rome was " 'anti-Christ, the proud, worldly priest of Rome, and the most cursed of clippers and cut-purses.' "[5] In 1377 the Pope condemned Wylcif's writings as heretical and of danger to the church and state. However, Pope Gregory died shortly thereafter, and no further notice was given to his threatening bulls.

The issue that ultimately brought Wylcif into condemnation with the papacy was his view concerning the papacy's right to own property. This was an economic factor; thus, the papacy considered it serious. It was in this area that Wylcif was in agreement with the Francisian Order. He claimed that all property was held on the principle of giving service to God and being in fellowship with Him. In theory all righteous men owned land. The "Morning Star" left his ideas at mere theory and did not strive to implement them into practical measures. This would occur later in the Peasant Revolt of 1381. However, it was through Wyclif's ringing appeals that many considered the injustice of the papacy. Wylcif claimed:

> 'Secular lordships, that clerks have full falsely against God's law and spend so wickedly, shulden be given by the King and witty lords to poor gentlemen that wulden justly govern the

MEDIEVAL CHRISTIANITY: THE FEUD

people, and maintain the land against enemies.'[6]

At the accession of Richard II, Wyclif was a very controversial figure. He became friends with those of high prominence, including John of Gaunt. However, professors at Oxford ceased to support him.[7] After this occurred, Wyclif was confined to Lutterworth. During this period, he wrote a very important theological work called the *Trialogus*. It declared that if Scripture and the church do not agree, one must obey the Bible. Wyclif also set forth the principle that no Christian has the right to follow any man except as he emulates Christ. In December 1384 as Wyclif was saying mass, he had a stroke and died two years later.[8]

The judgment of the church hierarchy toward Wyclif was summoned up in these words by Walsingham, chronicler of St. Alvans:

'On the feast of the passion of St. Thomas of Canterbury, John de Wyclif, that instrument of the devil, that enemy of the Church, that author of confusion to the common people ... being struck with the horrible judgment of God, was smitten with palsy....'[9]

The Lateran decree of 1413 claimed that Wyclif's books must be burned, and the Council of Constance ordered that his bones be dug up and burned. Fuller writes a very ironic outcome of this act:

'They burnt his bones to ashes and cast them into Swift, a neighboring brook running hard by. Thus this brook hath conveyed his ashes into Avon, Avon into Severn, Severn into the narrow seas, they into the main ocean. And thus the ashes of Wycliffe are the emblem of this doctrine, which now is dispersed the world over.'[10]

MEDIEVAL CHRISTIANITY: THE FEUD
NOTES ON JOHN WYCLIF

1. Norman F. Cantor, *Medieval History* (New York: The Macmillan Co., 1963), p. 582.

2. James Westfall Thompson and Edgar Nathaniel Johnson, *An Introduction to Medieval Europe* (New York: W.W. Norton and Co., Inc., 1937), pp. 978, 979.

3. Ibid., p. 979.

4. Carl Stephenson, *Mediaeval History* (New York: Harper & Brothers, 1935), p. 667.

5. Philip Schaff, *History of the Christian Church*, 8 vols. (Grand Rapids: William B. Eerdmans Publishing Co., 1910), 6:316.

6. Thompson, *Introduction to Medieval Europe*, p. 980.

7. Stephenson, *Medieval History*, p. 668.

8. Schaff, *History of the Christian Church*, pp. 322, 323.

9. Ibid., p. 324.

10. Ibid., p. 325.

TWENTY-ONE GREAT VOICES

⁊ ERASMUS ☞

Erasmus, more than any of his contemporaries, set the stage for the Reformation. He was a humanist, but he was the epitome of anti-papal thought and is today considered to be both a child of the Middle Ages and modern times.

Erasmus lived between 1466 and 1536. He combined classical and Biblical learning coupled with sharp wit and a suaveness that was practically nonexistent in such an age. His great role would be to reinstate Christian antiquity. He set the wheels of the Reformation by satirizing many of the ecclesiastical abuses. He is today considered the first editor of the Greek New Testament which made it possible for Luther and Tyndale to make translations from the original. Many of his exegetical works are still considered brilliant today.[1] However, Erasmus was seemingly intoxicated not by Biblical studies so much as in the general revival of learning. In 1517 he wrote:

> 'All over the world, as if on a given signal splendid talents are stirring and awakening and conspiring together to revive the best learning. For what else is this but a conspiracy, when all these great scholars from different lands ... set about this noble task.'[2]

Erasmus was born out of wedlock to a Dutch priest. At a young age his displayed unusual signs of a splendid memory. Between the years 1486 and 1491, he was placed in a monastery and emerged from the experience with an intense hatred of monkery. However, it was during these years that he diligently studied classics. In 1492 he was ordained to the priesthood, but he never held a parish. In 1500 he traveled to England and became close friends with Sir Thomas More and Dean Colet. The latter influenced him to emphasize the Scriptures over scholasticism.[3] However, More highly extolled Erasmus' New Testament. Erasmus strongly believed that the Scriptures should only be read in the original languages, but he also realized for many this was too idealistic. He penned:

> 'I utterly disagree with those who do not want the Holy Scriptures to be read by the uneducated in their own language, as though Christ's teaching was so obscure that it could hardly be understood even by a handful of theologians.... I wish that every little woman could read the Gospel and the Epistles of Paul.'[4]

Erasmus was critical of scholastic jargon since he felt it obscured the simple teachings of the Word. However, Erasmus felt a kinship with the ideas of many of the great philosophers. He loved both Plato's philosophy and Christ's teachings. Sensing a great discrepancy between the plainness of Christ's teachings and the grandeur of the papal court, he wrote *Julius Exclusus,* a satirical work portraying Pope Julius II as being excluded from heaven. Erasmus did not wish to break with the church but to reform it. He also challenged the belief that religious truth is possible for many only by exercise of the rational faculties. He continued through his life to claim that education would subdue ignorance. Luther and Erasmus differed at this point; the former looked back to the classical era whereas the latter to the original spirit of Christianity. However, Erasmus greatly employed his love for classicism to study the Scriptures. He wrote: "

'If there is any fresh Greek to be had, I had rather pawn my coat than not get it, especially if it is something Christian, as the Psalms in Greek or the Gospels.' "[5] In words characteristic of Erasmus, he wrote:

> 'The strange and often confused [terms of the Bible], the metaphors and oblique figures of speech hold so much difficulty that we often perspire with effort before we understand the meaning.... It would be best if some men of piety ... were assigned the task of distilling from the purest sources ... the essence of the whole philosophy of Christ!' [6]

Erasmus clearly saw the evil of the abuses of the church and strove to turn theology back from the study of scholasticism to Scriptural study. His greatest work manifesting anticlericalism was the *Praise of Folly*. An excerpt of it reads:

> 'As to these Supreme Pontiffs who take the place of Christ ... if ever they thought upon the title of Pope - that is, Father - or the addition "Most Holy"' who on earth would be more afflicted? ... were wisdom to descend upon them, how it would inconvenience them! Wisdom did I say? Nay, even a grain of salt would do it.'[7]

However, Erasmus lacked true insight into the doctrine of grace. He had many tendencies that are peculiar to unorthodox theologians. He claimed there are many difficulties in the Scriptures. He omitted a verse in I John 5 since Erasmus could not find it in any manuscript. After a great debate he said he would include the verse if it could be found in one manuscript. A false manuscript was manufactured and included the verse.[8] He also doubted that John 8:1-11 was genuine. Many suspected him of teaching a type of Arianism. He did not emphasize the theme of humanity sinning in Adam and he defended human freedom. He also felt that many of the pagan classical writers were influenced in a similar manner as the Biblical authors.[9]

Luther and Erasmus had at one time been close friends. However after their controversy over the will and its freedom, they became bitter enemies. Luther claimed Erasmus was a "refined Epicurean, a modern Lucian, a disguised atheist, and enemy of all religion."[10]

We must give credit to Erasmus for his comprehension of Scripture with the small amount of light he possessed because of the period in which he lived. Erasmus is a central figure in church history even though he had many contradictory Christian characteristics and embraced humanistic elements. Primarily he is significant because he greatly influenced Luther of the necessity of getting to the original languages of the Scriptures.

MEDIEVAL CHRISTIANITY: THE FEUD

NOTES ON ERASMUS

1. Philip Schaff, *History of the Christian Church*, 8 vols. (Grand Rapids: William B. Eerdmans Publishing Co., 1910), 7:402, 403.

2. Roland Bainton, *Studies on the Reformation* (Boston: Beacon Press, 1963), p. 6.

3. Schaff, *History of the Christian Church*, pp. 405, 406.

4. *Opera*, LB, V. 141F, quoted in E. Harris Harbison, *The Christian Scholar* (New York: Charles Scribner's Sons, 1956), p. 100.

5. Samuel Stumpf, *Socrates to Sartre* (New York: McGraw-Hill Book Co., 1966), p. 221.

6. Letter to Paul Volz, Aug. 14, 1518 quoted in Bainton, *Studies on the Reformation*, p. 101.

7. *The Praise of Folly* quoted in Karl H. Dannenfeldt, *The Church of the Renaissance and Reformation* (St. Louis: Concordia Publishing House, 1970), p. 126.

8. Bainton, *Studies on the Reformation*, p. 8.

9. Schaff, *History of the Christian Church*, pp. 413, 414.

10. Ibid., p. 434.

TWENTY-ONE GREAT VOICES

3

Reformation Christianity: The Faction

TWENTY-ONE GREAT VOICES

❦ MARTIN LUTHER ❦

Martin Luther was born November 10, 1483 at Eisleben in Prussian Saxony. His early days were difficult as both parents believed in stern discipline. While very young he was taught many frightful tales about the devil and witches, and such stories would characterize his imagination throughout his life. The many hardships he faced as a youth expressed themselves in his later life. His lack of cultivation narrowed his influence among the higher classes but increased his popularity among the lower classes. He would always be associated with the people and not a particular elite group.

> He was not a polished diamond, but a rough block cut out from a granite mountain and well fitted for a solid base of a mighty structure. He laid the foundation, and others finished the upper stories.[1]

Luther obtained his Bachelor of Arts degree in 1502 and his Master of Arts in 1505. Then came a drastic turning point in his life. On July 17, 1505, he entered the Augustinian monastery at Erfurt. During these three years he was terribly troubled by the thought of his sin. He passed many lonely nights on his knees seeking to find peace of mind and settle the question of his eternal destiny. Luther declared," 'If a monk ever reached heaven by monkery, I would have found my way there also.' "[2]

Luther assumed very menial tasks to contain his pride. During this period he believed in the immaculate conception of Mary, and also confessed his sins weekly to a priest. However, the monastery offered no peace to Luther, thus, he still possessed the ever-present dread of sin in his life. Gradually, Luther began to comprehend the distinction between faith and works. He came to realize righteousness is not obtained by human effort, but that it abides in Christ and can only be a gift from Him. Luther came to this realization by the aid of Johann Von Staupitz. When Luther finally realized the nature of grace, he felt immeasurably relieved of his load of guilt.[3]

In 1508 Luther was appointed professor of theology at the University of Wittenberg where he was recognized as one of the leading professors. He was also known as a great preacher. During the period of his days of teaching at the university, Luther began to question the validity of the indulgence system.

> Many others felt equally strong about the scandal of indulgences, and many had spoken forcefully about the general need for reform in the church. The posting of Luther's theses is important only to hindsight, because it was the first, relatively moderate step which proved to be the point where Luther's path began to diverge sharply from Catholicism.[4]

Beginning in 1517, Pope Leo X would implement any measure to obtain money for maintenance of St. Peter's Cathedral at Rome. In order to obtain money he instituted on a large scale the sale of indulgences. Those who sold such were dispatched to various countries. John Tetzel came to Germany. As Luther pondered the reason for the sale of indulgences, he came to the conclusion it was an abomination to all. He believed the system to be totally unscriptural; thus, he was compelled to write his world renowned Ninety-Five Theses, which he nailed to the door of the castle church at Wittenberg on All Saints Day, October 31, 1517. Essentially the theses claimed there was no human mediator between God and man. He also stated one must be penitent in order to be forgiven by God. The direct effect of his theses was the Leipzig debate.[5]

The famous Leipzig debate occurred in 1519. Originally Carlstadt and John Eck confronted one another, but soon Luther was drawn into the debate. They debated many topics, but the papacy was the primary concern. Luther resorted to history and Scripture to substantiate his arguments, the primary one being the Bishop of Rome had been instituted only a few hundred years prior to the sixteenth century, and the early church did not recognize the office. Eck managed to force Luther into admitting he had Hussite tendencies. This admission proved damaging to Luther because Huss had been condemned years before, and Luther's association with Huss placed him in a questionable position. Eck had in a sense won the debate, but Luther would in the future be a dominant figure embodying the German national sentiments. After this debate, Luther began to realize that his attack on indulgences was aimed directly at the very heart of the role of the priest.[6]

Luther held Scripture in high esteem. He claimed the Holy Scriptures had been preserved by direct action of God. He did not ridicule human works, but the Bible was considered supreme to Luther. He claimed its internal characteristics rather than outward signs attested to its heavenly authenticity.

> 'The great, fine and useful books of Homer, Virgil and the like are ancient books; but they are nothing when compared with the Bible.... They regard only present things.... In short the

Holy Scriptures are the highest and best book of God, full of comfort in all tribulation.[7]

Luther claimed that the knowledge of the original languages was essential to understand and convey the true meaning of Scripture. He went so far as to state that this knowledge was an instrument of the Holy Spirit. He believed one must approach the Scriptures with a childlike mind and minimized the use of reason. Even though Luther regarded the Bible as inspired by God Himself, he admitted there was a very striking human quality to it. He claimed every book mirrored the author's human idiosyncrasies.[8]

Luther questioned the authenticity of James and Revelation. Of the latter he wrote:

> 'In this book there are wanting more things than one to make one believe it is neither apostolic or prophetic.... Many of the fathers of the church long ago rejected this book. Finally let every one think of it as his own mind inclines him, my mind can take no pleasure in the book.[9]

How did Luther arrive at his high esteem of the Scriptures? It was mainly through the influence of Erasmus. Erasmus' New Testament was published in 1516, and it was this text that Luther used to translate the Bible into German. After Luther wrote his Ninety-Five Theses, most scholars tended to think of him as another Erasmus. Martin Bucer wrote concerning Luther:

> 'He agrees with Erasmus in all things but with the difference in his favor, that what Erasmus only insinuates he teaches openly and freely....He has brought it all about that at

Wittenberg the ordinary textbooks have all been abolished, while the Greeks, and Jerome, and Augustine, and Paul are publicly taught.[10]

Even though Luther admired Erasmus, he was torn between admiration and suspicion of him. Luther believed Erasmus had no concept of the distinction between law and grace. Luther did in a sense repudiate any connection with Erasmus. In the spring of 1517 Luther wrote concerning Erasmus: " ' I fear he does not sufficiently advance the cause of Christ and God's grace... for human considerations weigh with him more than divine.' "[11]

Luther ignited the Germanic hatred of the papacy and has been credited with initiating the reformation of the church in that area. However even though Luther was a godly man and realized his strength came only from the Spirit of God, he still manifested characteristics of the flesh. In 1527 he wrote to a friend: " ' For more than a week I was close to the gates of death and hell. I trembled in all my members, Christ was wholly lost. I was shaken by desperation and blasphemy of God.' " [12] In spite of his inconsistencies Luther was used to awaken many to the necessity of a restoration of Biblical doctrine.

NOTES ON MARTIN LUTHER

1. Philip Schaff, *History of the Christian Church*, 8 vols. (Grand Rapids: William B. Eerdmans Publishing Co., 1910), 7:109.

2. *Opera XXXI,* p. 273, quoted in William Stevenson, *The Story of the Reformation* (Richmond: John Knox Press, 1959), p. 301.

3. Schaff, *History of the Christian Church*, 7:113-119.

4. Henry Brinton, *The Context of the Reformation* (London: Hutchinson Educational Ltd., 1968), p. 86.

5. Stevenson, *The Story of the Reformation*, pp. 32-34.

6. Ibid., pp. 36-37.

7. *Reliquien,* no page given, quoted in K. R. Hagenbach, *History of the Reformation in Germany and Switzerland Chiefly*, 2 vols. (Edinburgh: T & T Clark, 1878), 2:154.

8. Hagenbach, *History of the Reformation,* 2:157.

9. Ibid., 2;160.

10. *Luther's Correspondence,* Ep. 57, quoted in E. Harris Harbison, *The Christian Scholar in the Age of Reformation* (New York: Charles Scribner's Sons, 1956), p. 104.

11. *Luther's Correspondence*, Ep. 21, quoted in E. Harris Harbison, *The Christian Scholar in the Age of the Reformation,* p. 106.

12. R. H. Borhmer, *Road to Reformation* (Philadelphia: Muhlenberg Press, 1946), p. 288.

⁊ ULRICH ZWINGLI ⁊

Ulrich Zwingli was born on January 1, 1484, only two months after the birth of Luther. He was exposed to a Catholic education which emphasized humanistic studies. When he was only ten years old, he was sent to a Latin school in Basel and studied such diverse subjects as grammar, music, and dialectics. Between 1500 and 1502 he was a student at the University of Vienna. Here he concentrated on scholastic philosophy and physics but primarily ancient classics. In 1506 he obtained the degree of Master of Arts; however, he never acquired the doctorate as did Luther. Zwingli was ordained by the Bishop of Constance and became the pastor of Glarus. He maintained his position there between 1506 and 1516. During this period he diligently studied Greek in order to be able to understand the New Testament in the original language.[1] During Zwingli's tenure in Glarus, he had a close friend named Glareanus who described him as " ' the greatest philosopher and theologian.' "[2]

In 1516 Zwingli was called by Baron Theobald von Geroldseck to Einsiedeln, which was a secluded section encircled by numerous mountains. In Einsiedeln Zwingli began his career of preaching. He clearly preached Christ and the Scriptures. One contemporary witness of Zwingli and his time at Einsiedeln said:

> 'To stand amist the throngs of pious pilgrims and preach the gospel to them, and especially to influence many a man of the higher classes through the power of the Word of God, was

the task of Zwingli in Einsiedeln.... On Whitsunday of 1518 he preached on the man with the palsy. Amongst his auditors was Caspar Hedio.... In a beautiful ... impressive, and wholly evangelical manner, it brought home to him the spirit and power of the old theology.'[3]

While at Einsiedeln, Zwingli had no intentions of breaking with Rome. He was at this period a humanist and desired to improve the church from within. However, in retrospect in 1522 he wrote:

'My connection with the pope of Rome is now a thing of several years back. At the time it began it seemed to me a proper thing to take his money and to defend his opinions, but when I realized my sin I departed company with him entirely.'[4]

In December 1518, Zwingli was called as pastor of the Great Minster Cathedral of Zurich, and it was here that he proclaimed many of his ideas of reform. He especially preached against purgatory and celibacy. In January 1523, he drew up and defended his sixty-seven theses. They were broader than Luther's, and their stress was the sufficiency of Christ's death for complete salvation. He also harangued the Roman Catholic system.[5]

Even though Luther and Zwingli agreed on the means of salvation by Christ alone apart from the church, they disagreed on many issues which had the effect of causing a rift between the two. In 1529 Zwingli and Luther met at Marburg to establish a common ground between them in order to present the "faith" in a united effort. They agreed on fourteen of the fifteen points discussed. The point they could never harmonize was the mass. Luther held a view between that of Catholic transubstantiation and the symbolic view of later Protestants. Zwingli held to the latter view. From the disagreement of the mass their rift grew larger as they disputed the two natures of Christ.[6]

Zwingli's theology and works formed the basis for evangelical Reformed theology. He accepted the orthodox views of the Trinity and the divine-human quality of Christ. His theology consisted of rational supernaturalism which was opposed to Luther's mysticism. He adhered to such orthodox thought as Scripture being the final authority on matters of salvation. Christ is the only means of salvation and as such there is no need for a human mediator between man and God.

Zwingli adhered firmly to God's election as the means of man's salvation. He was in many respects a forerunner of Calvin because he began with the principle of the absolute sovereignty of God. He claimed that foreknowledge and foreordination were synonymous. He claimed that God is the cause of every thing, and even the fall of Adam is part of His eternal plan. Election is free and is not contingent upon faith but involves faith. One can be saved without baptism but not without Christ. One is elected so that one can believe in Christ. Those who hear and reject the word are predestinated to eternal damnation. Zwingli stressed that all children of believing parents who die are also elected to eternal life. He claimed there was hope for those outside the church because God's grace is infinite; this aspect of Zwingli's differed from any other reformer.[7]

Zwingli was killed in the Second War of Cappel. It was declared that his body was to be quartered for treason and burned. His ashes were then scattered in the wind.

NOTES ON ULRICH ZWINGLI

1. Philip Schaff, *History of the Christian Church*, 8 vols. (Grand Rapids: William B. Eerdmans Publishing Co., 1910), 7:21-23.

2. Ibid., p. 25.

3. Morikofer, Vol. I, p. 39 quoted in K. R. Hagenbach, *History of the Reformation in Germany and Switzerland Chiefly*, 2 vols. (Edinburgh: T & T Clark, 1878), 2:239.

4. Harry E. Fosdick, *Great Voices of the Reformation* (New York: Random House, 1952), p. 159.

5. Karl H. Dannenfeldt, *The Church of the Renaissance and Reformation* (St. Loius: Concordia Publishing House, 1970), pp. 62, 63.

6. Henry Briton, *The Context of the Reformation* (London: Hutchinson Educational Ltd., 1968), pp. 94, 95.

7. Schaff, *History of the Christian Church*, p. 91-93.

⁊ JOHANN HEINRICH BULLINGER ⁊

Johann Heinrich Bullinger in December 1531 became Zwingli's able successor. His duties in Zurich were those of a Bishop having charge over a synod which he himself organized. Also during this period, he reformed the school system and initiated a central system for the money acquired from cloister lands.[1] His role in the Swiss Reformation was that of providing stability during a time of great difficulty. Bullinger was well equipped for this task since he was a man of faith and endurance.

Bullinger was born in Bremgarten and was the youngest of the five sons of Dean Bullinger. His father disdained the sale of indulgences, and he adhered to Reformation doctrine. Johann Bullinger was educated in the school of the Brethren of Common Life, which was located at the University of Cologne. He began to study scholastic theology but became attracted to Scripture primarily by the influence of Luther's and Melanchthon's writings. After securing his Master of Arts degree, he returned to Switzerland and was a professor in the Cistercian Convent at Cappel between 1523 and 1529. It was during this period that he met Zwingli.[2]

At this time the leadership in Zurich, under Zwingli's direction, was determined to make it possible for all the cantons to have free preaching. The citizens of the Protestant cantons stopped selling grain and steel to the Catholics, and this action resulted in a war between the two. Zwingli was killed in the battle that was fought on

October 11, 1531, at Cappel, and Bullinger was chosen to fill Zwingli's vacancy.[3]

Bullinger did not become involved with politics because he had seen that this had proved fatal for Zwingli. He believed there should exist a friendly relationship between church and state. He confined himself to the job of preacher and teacher, and his sermons were clear and practical providing an excellent model for younger preachers. In his first years he preached six to seven times each week. However, this pace began to prove too strenuous for him. He wrote:

> 'I am overwhelmed with the tasks of continuous and arduous preaching and there are also lectures to be given. I have to devote several hours to this or that friend, now writing letters, now giving advice to someone who has come specially to see me. As well as this I want to preach the message of Christ to people who are far away....This is why I am preparing some commentaries for preaching.... There is little time left for eating, sleeping, and refreshing the body and the soul.'[4]

Bullinger had a first-hand knowledge of the English Reformation primarily because many had fled to Zurich during Mary's reign. Archbishop Cramner invited Bullinger to a conference in London. The influence of the Reformed theology under Elizabeth was primarily because of Bullinger's impact.[5]

Bullinger adhered to the doctrine of the Reform church against the Roman Catholics and Lutherans. His beliefs were those of the Reformed faith intermingled with a moderate Calvinism. He had a different view of the sacrament than Zwingli. Bullinger tended to see the elements of the sacrament as possessing the spiritual presence of Christ, whereas Zwingli believed it was only memorial. He opposed the Anabaptists as did Zwingli. He consented to Servetus' death, yet Bullinger was not a man of violence.[6]

Bullinger had an Augustinian view of God but remained an opponent of Calvin. Bullinger and Thomas Erastus sought to prevent the expansion of Presbyterian government into the Rhineland and gave the English bishops his support against Thomas Cantwright's Presbyterian viewpoint.[7]

On August 26, 1575, Bullinger asked all the professors of theology and the pastors of his city to come listen to him while he lay in his death bed. He gave many warnings against envy, hatred, and lack of self control. He died about three weeks after this event and was buried at the Great Minster beside his wife and friend Peter Martyr.[8]

NOTES ON JOHANN HEINRICH BULLINGER

1. J. D. Douglas, ed., *The New International Dictionary of the Christian Church* (Grand Rapids: Zondervan Publishing House, 1974), p. 165.

2. Philip Schaff, *History of the Christian Church,* 8 vols. (Grand Rapids: William B. Eerdmans Publishing Co., 1910), 7:205.

3. Edward Hulme, *The Protestant Revolution and the Catholic Reformation* (New York: The Century Co., 1915), pp. 274-275.

4. Henri Daniel-Rops, *The Protestant Reformation* (London: J. M. Dent and Sons Ltd., 1961), p. 482.

5. Schaff, *History of the Christian Church,* pp. 208, 209.

6. Ibid., p. 209-211.

7. Douglas, *New International Dictionary,* p. 165.

8. Schaff, *History of the Christian Church,* p. 213.

⚜ WILLIAM FAREL ⚜

Zwingli was not the sole reformer from Switzerland. There was a man who had the appellations "The Elijah of the Reformation" and "The Scourge of the Priests." His name was William Farel. He had at one time been a promoter of the papacy only to later condemn it as a corrupt and abusive system. He especially loathed the pope and was not above calling him an antichrist. He also detested icons and advocated their destruction.

William Feral was born in 1489 to a wealthy family in Gap of Dauphine. When he embraced Protestantism, Farel was expelled from France and welcomed to Switzerland primarily because of his outstanding ability as a preacher.[1] He was never ordained but still possessed the belief that God had divinely appointed him to proclaim the truths of the Word. Farel was not an amiable person but rather a born fighter. Once he was fired at by a priest and the gun exploded. Turning around, Farel replied, "I am not afraid of your shots." Though he did not believe that physical violence was in accord with Scripture, he readily resorted to haranguing and verbally expressing views against the papacy. Farel had an unusual amount of endurance, and persecution and criticism served only as a stimulus to encourage him further in his work.[2] "Yet Farel did not limit himself to denunciation. He understood well, and knew how to inculcate eloquently the distinctive doctrines of the Protestant faith."[3]

His greatest gift was that of an orator. He was an articulate speaker who made excellent use of gestures. He also appeared to be very earnest and commanded attention from his audience. Nothing today remains of his sermons, but many claim that the real power was not in the content but in the manner in which he delivered his sermons.

> Farel was a strange little man, rather like a red gnome with a face riddled with scarlet pimples, bloodshot eyes, and enormous lips. Whether he was talking to a large crowd or a single listener, his voice was always sharply pitched; the veins in this neck would swell, and he gave the permanent impression of haranguing or censuring. He was also highly intelligent: he gauged his own limitations with perfect accuracy, and desired for himself only the humble but necessary place of John the Baptist alongside a new Messiah.[4]

Farel studied at Paris and mainly pursued ancient languages, philosophy and theology. His primary professor, Jacques Le Fevre d'Etaples, impressed on him the importance of the doctrine of justification by faith. Farel took his Master of Arts in 1517 and was a lecturer at the College of Cardinal.

By means of personal Bible study and the influence of Le Fevre, Farel gradually came to the conclusion that it is only through Christ that one can obtain salvation, and that the traditions of Rome were fallacious. He was astonished when he could not find in Scripture any mention of purgatory, the seven sacraments, indulgences or the papal hierarchy. In 1523, he fled to Basal and was housed by Oecolampadius. The suggestion of the latter led Farel to hold a disputation in Latin on his thirteen theses. These promoted justification by faith and denounced the papacy. He also spoke many times in

Basel. He was soon driven from the city mainly because Erasmus considered him a dangerous disturber of the peace. The year 1528 found Farel in many cities as an itinerate preacher. He would preach any place, and always his words made people either loathe or love what he said. Many times priests, women and monks would spit on Farel and threaten him with death. In December 1529, he brought the spirit of the Reformation to Neuchatel and neighboring cities.[5]

In December 1533, Farel went to Geneva. The Catholics were still in the majority, but during the following months the impact of his preaching reversed the situation entirely. Geneva became a Protestant city. In 1535 under Farel's influence, the Church of La Madeleine and the Cathedral of St. Peter were seized and an iconoclastic movement swept throughout the city. The General Assembly of Geneva on May 21, 1536, made Protestantism its official religion. Soon Calvin came to the city, and after a heated discussion Farel convinced him to join the movement.[6]

Farel's main defect was that he was not tactful or discreet. He had a tendency to bring opposition upon himself that could have easily been avoided. Oecolampadius wrote to Farel and said," 'Your mission is to evangelize, not to curse. Prove yourself to be an evangelist, not a tyrannical Legislator. Men want to be led, not driven.' "[7] Farel's work was primarily that of a preacher, not a theologian. He would pass his efforts to Calvin, and Feral was willing to support him fully. When hearing of Calvin's death in 1564, Farel wrote to Fabri: " 'Would I could die for him! What a beautiful course he has happily finished.' "[8]

Farel died September 13, 1565, at the age of seventy-six. A monument was placed in 1876 at Neuchatel to commemorate his work there. Most of his works and tracts have not been translated from French.

REFORMATION CHRISTIANITY: THE FACTION

NOTES ON WILLIAM FAREL

1. George P. Fisher, T*he Reformation* (London: Charles Scribner's Sons, 1906), p. 183.

2. Philip Schaff, *History of the Christian Church*, 8 vols. (Grand Rapids: William B. Eerdmans Publishing Co., 1910), p. 237.

3. Fisher, *The Reformation*, p. 183.

4. Henri Daniel-Rops, *The Protestant Reformation* (London: J. M. Dent and Sons, Ltd., 1961) p. 393.

5. Schaff, *History of the Christian Church,* pp. 239-242.

6. B. K. Kuiper, *The Church in History* (Grand Rapids: William B. Eerdmans Publishing Co., 1964), pp. 192, 193.

7. Schaff, *History of the Christian Church,* p. 238.

8. Ibid., p. 249.

TWENTY-ONE GREAT VOICES

☙ JOHN CALVIN ❧

John Calvin is widely recognized as one of the Church's greatest theologians. He was born July 10, 1509, at Noyon in the province of Picardy. His father was stern, and he was acquainted with the better families of the province. Calvin received his primary education with the de Mommor family, and by association with this family he obtained refined and aristocratic mannerisms. His father's sole desire for his precocious son was to enter the legal profession. At eighteen years of age Calvin was assigned the charge of Saint Martin de Marteville; however, on April 20, 1529, he traded the duties of Saint Martin for the Pont-L'Eveque. Since he was not ordained, he did not give the sacraments, but only preached. Money obtained from his duties there made it possible for him to attend the College de La Marche in 1523. Here he studied grammar and rhetoric. He was shortly transferred to the ecclesiastical College de Montague and studied philosophy and theology at this school.[1]

Calvin received the best education France had to offer, and he concentrated in the humanities, law and philosophy. From 1528 to 1533 he studied in three universities - Orleans, Bourges, and Paris. As long as his father was living he pursued the study of law, but upon his death Calvin again with renewed vigor began the study of the humanities and theology. His professors considered him one of their peers rather than an auditor. However, because of such laborious studying, Calvin's health began to suffer and throughout his life he experienced headaches and insomnia. His primary teacher in Greek and Hebrew was Melchior Volmar. Calvin spent hours discussing the Reformation with him. Volmar had been a pupil of LeFevre; thus, we see Calvin, as Zwingli, began as a humanist. Both admired Erasmus and the classics, but both looked primarily to God's wisdom.[2]

Calvin, unlike Augustine, had not lived a self-indulgent life before his conversion. Rather, he had been devoted to the Catholic religion and was looked upon as possessing an unblemished character. No pastor or friend led him to Christ. Rather, it was in the still of his study. Calvin wrote:

> 'But God by the secret guidance of his providence, at length gave a different direction to my course. And first, since I was too obstinately devoted to the superstitions of the Popery to be easily extricated from so profound an abyss of mire, and by a sudden conversion subdued and brought my mind to a teachable frame, which was more hardened in such matters than might have been expected from one at my early period of life. Having thus received some taste and knowledge of true godliness, I was immediately inflamed with so intense a desire to make progress therein....'[3]

Calvin came under the suspicion of the Parisian authorities, and after wandering for some time he went to Basal in 1535. It was in this city the following year that he wrote one of the most respected of Reformation works, *The Institutes of the Christian Religion.* In 1536 he went to Geneva and took a position as teacher in the church of Geneva. Calvin wrote: " 'Farel kept me at Geneva, not so much by advice and entreaty as by a dreadful adjuration, as if God had stretched forth his hand upon me from on high to arrest me.' "[4]

Reformation Christianity: The Faction

Many believed Calvin was too legalistic in his new position in Geneva. In 1537, Calvin and Farel passed an ordinance stating the Lord's Supper had to be celebrated at certain periods, congregational singing was to be instituted, and children were to learn a catechism. Both Farel and Calvin also introduced a confession of faith, but soon a dispute resulted, and both were exiled in 1538.

Between 1538 and 1541 Calvin preached and taught theology in Strasbourg. He married Idelette du Bure in 1540, but they were married only nine years as she died in 1549. Calvin's son also died.[5] He wrote:

> 'The Lord gave me a son and he hath taken him away again; let them my adversaries regard my affliction as a disgrace, if it please them to do so. Cannot I count my sons by tens of thousands throughout the Christian world?'[6]

Calvin returned to Geneva in September 1541 and stayed there until May 7, 1564. He preached his last sermon on February 6, 1564, and on April 2 he received the sacrament for the last time from Beza. Beza wrote concerning Calvin's death:

> 'I had just left him a little before, and on receiving intimation from the servants, immediately hastened to him with one of the brethren. We found that he had already died, and so very calmly.... Indeed he looked much more like one sleeping than dead.'[7]

Calvin's doctrinal system has had an unprecedented impact upon not only theology but also many other disciplines. At the focal point of his theology is the sovereignty of God which is best expressed in acrostic "tulip." The five points are total depravity of all people, unconditional election, limited atonement, irresistible grace, and the perseverance of the saints.[8] His system of theology can be subdivided into four branches: the establishment of the true "status questionis," or the points of dispute; second, examination of Scripture in favor of Calvinism which opposes Arminianism; third, the objection of the Arminians against Calvin's beliefs; and last, Calvinism applied in a practical manner.[9] This application found expression mainly in the encouragement of education and the stimulation of capitalism.

REFORMATION CHRISTIANITY: THE FACTION

NOTES ON JOHN CALVIN

1. Philip Schaff, *History of the Christian Church*, 8 vols. (Grand Rapids: William B. Eerdmans Publishing Co., 1910), 8:297, 301-302.

2. Ibid., pp. 304, 305, 309.

3. *Psalms*, pp. 40, 41, cr. 59, 21-23 quoted in Hans J. Hillebrand, *The Reformation* (New York: Harper and Row Publishers, 1964), p. 176.

4. Harry E. Fosdick, *Great Voices of the Reformation* (New York: Random House, 1952), p. 196.

5. Earle E. Cairns, *Christianity through the Centuries* (Grand Rapids: Zondervan Publishing House, 1954), pp. 337, 338.

6. K. R. Hagenbach, *History of the Reformation in Germany and Switzerland Chiefly*, 2 vols. (Edinburgh: T & T Clark, 1879), 2:319.

7. Schaff, *History of the Christian Church*, 8:823.

8. Cairns, *Christianity Through the Centuries*, pp. 336, 337.

9. William Cunningham, *The Reformers and the Theology of the Reformation* (Edinburgh: T & T Clark, 1866), p. 599.

TWENTY-ONE GREAT VOICES

⁑ THEODORE BEZA ⁑

Theodore Beza was born to Pierre and Marie Besze (the old French spelling) on June 24, 1519. He was born of a higher class than most reformers and because of this was respected by the noble class. His mother died when he was very young, and his father, believing himself inadequate to care for him, provided for Theodore to be partially adopted by Nicholas de Besze, a councilor in Paris' parliament. He provided the best teachers possible for the young boy he cherished. Theodore studied under Melchior Volmar, who also taught Calvin. Beza was twelve years old when he met Calvin. He would eventually become Calvin's right-hand man and successor of the Reformation in Geneva.[1]

Theodore's uncle died in 1532, and he was looked after by Claudius, the abbot of the Cisteruan monastery of Froimont. This abbot and Theodore's father had strong desires to see that the young man pursued the study of law; therefore, they sent him to the University of Orleans. He studied diligently and in 1539 took the degree of Licentiate of the Law. However, after many heated debates, Beza convinced his father that he should not pursue his studies in law but rather in literature. It was during this period that he wrote many poems, and in 1548 they were published in his famous collection *Juvenilia*. The work was acclaimed as superior and ranked him as one of the great Latin poets. It never occurred to him that anyone would ever censor his poems, but many did, especially when he became associated with the Protestant cause. Many began to read between the lines and accused him of sensuous innuendos. Beza claimed until his death he had no such intentions. Also, during the period of the writing of his poems he secretly married Claudine Denosse, and Beza promised he would later publicly marry her. In 1548 he became seriously ill and was at the brink of death. His conscience bothered him for not speaking out about his Protestant convictions and his secret marriage. On October 23, 1548 he and Claudine crossed the border into Switzerland and traveled to Geneva. There he again met Calvin.[2]

Beza was a close friend during Calvin's later years. Beza, Calvin considered, was bright and was the best defender of this system of theology. He became after Calvin's death the most influential theologian of the Reformed faith and held such a position for forty years. His influence was felt in all countries that embraced the Reformed faith. He personally encouraged John Knox in the Reformed doctrines. He also did much to direct the views of Andrew Melille.[3]

In 1558 he became professor of Greek at Geneva. The next year Beza became rector and taught theology in the Genevan academy. However, he always kept a variety of interests. He published a history of the Reformed movement and his own text of the New Testament. He also served as advisor of the Huguenot movement.[4]

Beza had known for years that he was to be Calvin's successor. There had always existed a close relationship between the two based upon respect for one another. Beza gave Calvin his last sacrament before his death in 1564.[5] The leadership could not have been passed on to a more qualified man than Beza. He was inferior to Calvin in theological knowledge, but far surpassed him in knowledge and grace of courtly life and social customs. Under Beza the school of theology in Geneva became the center of continental Protestantism. Of the six great continental reformers - Luther, Melanchthon, Zwingli, Bullinger, Calvin and Beza - the latter was considered the most polished in manners.[6]

One of Beza's great contributions to Biblical scholarship was the *Codex Catabrigiensis,* a manuscript of the Gospels and Acts which dates from the sixth century. His *Life of Calvin* was written in French and translated into Latin by himself. Philip Schaff drew heavily upon the book for his own work. He also published in 1573 a volume entitled *Epistolarum Theologicarum.* The volume proved to be very popular, and a third edition was begun in 1697.[7]

Beza's works are controversial, that is, they were written out of controversial matters among the reformers; therefore, they are not as appealing to the general populace as, for example, some of Luther's commentaries. They did, however, greatly influence subsequent Protestant leaders.

> They occupy a very important place in a survey of the history of theological speculation at that important era; and in all of them certainly Beza has afforded abundant proof, that he was possessed of great talents and extensive erudition, and that he was fully qualified in all respects to expound and discuss the most profound and difficult questions in theology.[8]

NOTES ON THEODORE BEZA

1. B. K. Kuiper, *The Church in History* (Grand Rapids: William B. Eerdmans Publishing co., 1964), p. 199.

2. Philip Schaff, *History of the Christian Church*, 8 vols. (Grand Rapids: William B. Eerdmans Publishing Co., 1910), 8:249-251.

3. William Cunningham, *The Reformers and the Theology of the Reformation* (Edinburgh: T & T Clark, 1866), p. 346.

4. J. D. Douglas, ed., *The New International Dictionary of the Christian Church* (Grand Rapids: Zondervan Publishing House, 1974), p. 126.

5. K. R. Hagenbach, *History of the Reformation*, 2 vols. (Edinburgh: T & T Clark, 1879), 2:343.

6. Schaff, *History of the Christian Church,* 8:863, 870.

7. Ibid., 8:872-874.

8. Cunningham, *The Reformers and the Theology of the Reformation*, pp. 348-349.

⚜ IGNATIUS LOYOLA ⚜

Ignatius Loyola was born in 1491 into a middle class family. He was the youngest of the eight sons of Don Beltram Yanez Y Loyola. Even though they were not wealthy, their family was a proud one; two centuries earlier the family had been given a coat of arms by King Alfonso XII of Castile. One of Ignatius' brothers became a priest, but he himself decided to become a soldier. During this period his country was not engaged in war, and young Loyola spent his time in gambling, duels and love affairs. Hardly would anyone imagine that he would be the founder of the most renowned order of the Catholic Church, the Jesuit Order.

Loyola exhibited unusual courage as a young man. He once became extremely angry with a band of soldiers and chased after them alone with sword in hand. He again displayed his courage in his last moments as a soldier. In a battle against the French, he refused to surrender even though all the other officers wished to do so. Immediately after this decision, a cannon ball hit his right leg and shattered the bone. The incident had a profound effect on his life as it caused him to consider spiritual matters in a different light.[1]

After the fall of Pampeluna and during his recovery from his leg injury, Loyola's whole attitude toward life began to change. He wished no longer to be a soldier of the king, but rather one for Christ. He would begin to battle with weapons of the Spirit and desired to copy the deeds of the medieval saints. He lived a hermit-type life for three years, practicing extreme self-denial. However, he realized that he needed more education, especially in theology. He began to study Latin, and in 1528 he matriculated in the University of Paris where he stayed for seven years studying and gathering around him a band of disciples. He never became a great scholar, but he possessed qualities that made more learned men follow him. He had qualities of sincerity, determination and an ability to relate to people. His insight into the human personality was succinctly expressed in *Spiritual Exercises,* a book that helped to win followers and established the character of the order. The book was based on an introspective study of his own experience in the early days of his conversion. His book gave directions for intensive contemplation, and the work was designed to bring the reader into a spiritual experience. The book indeed did transform many into devoted soldiers of the church.[2]

Loyola wished to thwart the Protestant Reformation, and he attempted to find the means to counteract its progress. According to the constitution of his society, he alone possessed total authority. He endeavored to annihilate all personal freedom so all would be completely submissive to his desires. In order to accomplish obedience to himself and his society, he also desired to exclude the Pope's authority over the members of his society since they were bound by a constitution. The Pope gave Loyola permission for members of the order to become missionaries to the Holy Land. However, they were prevented from obtaining their goal of reaching Palestine because of the war between Charles V and the Turks.[3]

Loyola's desire was that the order should not only propagate Catholic doctrine, but it also should be beneficial to society at large. He believed in caring for those in the ghetto, caring for orphans, reforming of prostitutes, helping beggars and establishing schools. By

REFORMATION CHRISTIANITY: THE FACTION

1542, many of the society's preachers were ministering in northern Italy. Portugal was won to the society by 1542, and in France they began to make steady inroads. They were remarkably successful in Germany under the direction of Pierre Favre.[4]

Loyola's emphasis on efficiency was expressed by the military organization of the society and its many rules. New members were to be chosen carefully. The initiate had to possess intelligence, good appearance, pleasing personality, and excellent character. Before one could become a full member, he had to pass an extensive period of training. He then had to take the monastic vows of poverty, obedience and moral purity. There was also a select "inner circle" from which the officers were to be chosen.[5]

In 1548, Ignatius Loyola was proclaimed general of the Society of Jesus. He ruled the society with an iron hand. In 1551, he founded the Roman College which became a model school for the Jesuits. Soon the Jesuits led in the reformation of the Catholic church. The founder of the Society of Jesus died in 1556. However, his name lives on since he was beatified in 1609 and canonized in 1622.[6]

NOTES ON IGNATIUS LOYOLA

1. Theodore Maynard, *Saint Ignatius and the Jesuits* (New York: P.J. and Sons, 1956), pp. 17-20.

2. Wallace K. Ferguson and Geoffrey Bruun, *A Survey of European Civilization* (Boston: Houghton Mifflin Company, 1969), pp. 384, 385.

3. R.W. Thompson, *The Footprints of the Jesuits* (New York: Hunt and Eaton, 1894), pp. 36-40.

4. John Fulton, *The Epochs of Church History* (New York: Charles Scribner's Sons, 1901), pp. 379-380.

5. Ferguson and Bruun, *A Survey of European Civilization*, p. 386.

6. J. D. Douglas, ed., *The New International Dictionary of the Christian Church* (Grand Rapids: Zondervan Publishing House 1974), p. 499.

4

Late Christianity: The Faith

TWENTY-ONE GREAT VOICES

LATE CHRISTIANITY: THE FAITH

⚜ JOHN WESLEY ⚜

The founder of Methodism, John Wesley, was born June 17, 1703. At the age of six he was rescued from a burning rectory, and this event apparently had a profound effect upon him the rest of his life since he continually alluded to himself as " 'a brand snatched from the burning.'"[1] John was the fifteenth child of Samuel and Susanna Wesley. His parents belonged to the Anglican church, but his grandparents were Puritans. He was educated at Oxford, and in 1726 Wesley was elected to a fellowship at Lincoln College, which was one of the many colleges of Oxford. John Potter ordained him to the priesthood in 1728. He returned to Oxford to discover that his brother, Charles, had begun a Christian organization called the "Holy Club." They read Scripture and devotional literature and visited the sick. The group's counselor was William Law, and Wesley greatly admired him and sought his counsel many times.[2] During this period, Wesley considered becoming a hermit in order to live a life of contemplation. He was deeply influenced by Tauler and the *Theologia Germanica*. However, he finally decided to minister to American Indians.

In 1735 both Charles and John Wesley accepted an invitation to labor in Georgia; they stayed there for three years but found their ministry was unsuccessful. Wesley had been trained in England and his rigid professionalism clashed with the colonial parishioners. This situation ultimately led him to lose interest in mysticism. He had crossed the Atlantic with a group of Moravians, and as he observed their calmness on the sea during a bad storm; he saw the contrast between their trust and his anxiety during such a situation. Wesley knew he feared death, but he discovered that the Moravians did not because they claimed salvation by faith in Christ. He returned from Georgia in 1738 seeing the essential issue in salvation is that Christ alone is the one who saves.[3]

Wesley reminds us of the young Martin Luther because he was attempting to save himself by his good works. He always displayed Christian behavior, but he lacked joy in his life. He again met with some Moravians and a man named Peter Bohler. At a meeting in London he experienced a climatic point in his life. He was converted.

> 'In the evening I went very unwillingly to a society in Aldersgate Street where one was reading Luther's preface to the epistle to the Romans. About a quarter before nine, while he was describing the change which God works in the heart through faith in Christ, I felt my heart strangely warmed. I felt I did trust in Christ, Christ alone for my salvation; and an assurance was given me that he had taken away my sins, even mine, and saved me from the law of sin and of death.[4]

After his new birth, Wesley went to Herrnhut and met Count Zinzendort. He then returned to England and began his life endeavor - to bring Christ to the English nation. Wesley claimed he had only " 'one point of view - to promote so far as I am able vital, practical religion; and by the grace of God to beget, preserve, and increase the life of God in the souls of men.' "[5]

He began an unprecedented amount of preaching which affected the lives of the majority of Englishmen directly and indirectly. He appealed to individuals to personally receive Christ. He did much open-air preaching which was considered out of line by the Church of England. He soon recruited young George Whitefield, and both led extensive evangelistic meetings. Many times he had to overcome hostile crowds. He wrote of such a crowd:

> 'The winds were hushed and all was calm and still; my heart was filled with love, my eyes with tears and my mouth with arguments. They were amazed. They were ashamed. They were melted down. They devoured my every word,'[6]

Wesley had an unusual amount of energy. In unwearied preaching, he labored fifty years proclaiming Christ in churches, fields, and meeting houses. Many times his listeners would become very emotional, but Wesley never encouraged sentimentalism. He began to appoint lay preachers throughout the country. In 1744 the two Wesleys and four other clergymen, along with four laymen, defined their doctrine and established rules of conduct.[7]

Wesley did not break with the Anglican church but organized many small societies. These societies were divided and these in turn were also broken down. There was then a leader over each of these small groups. He also divided England into five circuits and ordained Thomas Coke as superintendent of the Methodist Church of America. It was after Wesley's death that the Methodist Church was established in England. Wesley was an Arminian in doctrine, and he broke with Whitefield who stressed, Wesley believed, Calvinism too strongly. Wesley stressed salvation by faith, but the fruit of this faith is love. This element, he believed, would after salvation expel the imperfections of the sinner's life.

Wesley desired his preaching to revolutionize English society. Thousands were converted through his efforts, and many claim he more than anyone had the most profound spiritual impact upon the English nation.[8]

LATE CHRISTIANITY: THE FAITH

NOTES ON JOHN WESLEY

1. Walker, *A History of the Christian Church* (New York: Charles Scribner's Sons, 1970), p. 456.

2. James H. Nichols, *History of Christianity* 1650-1950 (New York: The Ronald Press Co., 1956), pp. 87, 88.

3. Ibid., p. 88.

4. Harry E. Fosdick, *Great Voices of the Reformation* (New York: Random House, 1952), pp. 493, 494.

5. J. D. Douglas, ed., *The New International Dictionary of the Christian Church* (Grand Rapids: Zondervan Publishing House, 1974), p. 1034.

6. Fosdick, *Great Voices of the Reformation*, p. 495.

7. S. Cheetham, *A History of the Christian Church* (London: Macmillan and Co., Ltd., 1907), pp. 186, 187.

8. Earle Cairns, *Christianity through the Centuries* (Grand Rapids: Zondervan Publishing House, 1954), p. 418.

TWENTY-ONE GREAT VOICES

☙ GEORGE WHITEFIELD ❧

The Great Awakening was an eighteenth century religious movement that swept America. George Whitefield played an initial role in this religious revival. He came into the world on December 16, 1714. The son of a tavern keeper, George was surrounded by poverty and scenes of low morality. However, there was a school in Gloucester, and George prepared himself for college there.[1]

George attended the Free Grammar School of the city, and here he was a day student until his fifteenth year. The only facts that were recorded about his schooling there were that he was known for his elocution and his memory, and that he was appointed to recite speeches before the Corporation of Gloucester. He dropped out of school for three years, and at the age of eighteen entered Oxford University. He had lost interest in spiritual things two years before he went to Oxford, but upon entering Pembroke College he began to visit prisons and read to the prisoners. He met John Wesley and a close friendship was begun. However, at one period it seemed Whitefield was steadily becoming an ascetic or mystic, he began to fast and refused to powder his hair as was the custom.[2] A revolutionary change was about to occur; he was experienced conversion.

> Above all, my mind being now more open and enlarged, I began to read the Holy Scriptures upon my knees, laying aside all other books, and praying over, if possible, every line

and word. This proved meat indeed and drink indeed to my soul. I daily received fresh life, light and power from above. I got more true knowledge from reading the book of God in one month than I could ever have acquired from all the writings of men.[3]

When he finally grasped the truth he never again returned to his old ascetic way of life.

His first sermon was preached at the Church of St. Mary-le-Crypt, Gloucester. He was at first frightened by the large crowd that had gathered, but he reassured himself by remembering successful speeches in the past. He preached a sermon of such passion that a complaint was issued to the Bishop claiming that young Whitefield had driven fifteen people mad. After preaching in several London churches, he accepted an invitation from John and Charles Wesley to venture to Georgia.[4]

Whitefield would eventually make seven visits to America. He possessed an extraordinary eloquence that stirred great audiences not only in America but also in England, Scotland, and Wales. However, he preached predestination to such an extent that Wesley felt he could not unite any longer with Whitefield.[5]

Many historians claim it was Whitefield's work which initiated the First Great Awakening in America.

> George Whitefield was the chief agent in consolidating the many local revivals into one great movement.... Other itinerant preachers followed his example and fused in the Awakening a common consciousness through the separate colonies.[6]

Whitefield was indeed an unusual preacher.

> Whitefield has no dignity. He would even go so far as to rave, stare, foam and beat his breast. He wept and laughed and sang in the pulpit. He could stir up men's emotions and play upon them as upon the taut strings of a violin. And Massachusetts men loved it. They waited in the rain to hear him.[7]

After his return from the colonies, he soon realized his once highly regarded position in the eyes of the clergy had been lost. Many claimed that he was a fanatic, and that he stressed the need for regeneration too strongly. His sphere of influence within the Church of England began to rapidly diminish. The outcome of this was that Whitefield turned to open-air preaching. Realizing that the majority of the people were not attending any church, he decided to bring the gospel to them. He soon began to be known throughout England. Thousands congregated to hear Whitefield proclaim the gospel, a message which sharply contrasted with that of the Church of England. His journeys were laborious especially since Whitefield traveled to many areas that did not have roads. He visited Scotland fourteen times and was perhaps accepted there more graciously than in any other country. He crossed the Atlantic seven times. Twice Whitefield went to Ireland and was almost murdered by a mob.[8]

His last sermon was preached at the age of fifty-six at Exeter. He preached for two hours from II Corinthians 8:5. After the service he was extremely tired and rode to Newbury Port. There, after an attack of spasmodic asthma, he died before six the next morning.[9]

Whitefield constantly preached an evangelical message of humanity's sin and God's grace. Many have criticized him for lack of freshness and claimed that he did too much speaking and not enough study and preparation. However, he did make his sermons personal. He would constantly use the expression, "My Brethren, I beseech you." He was extremely dramatic. No one of his time equaled him in oratory and the ability to produce dramatic atmosphere. William Cowper said of George Whitefield: " 'He followed Paul - his zeal a kindred flame, his apostolic charity the same.' "[10]

LATE CHRISTIANITY: THE FAITH

NOTES ON GEORGE WHITEFIELD

1. B. K. Kuiper, *The Church in History* (Grand Rapids: William B. Eerdmans Publishing Co., 1964), p. 345.

2. J. M. C. Ryle, *The Christian Leaders of the Last Century* (London: T. Nelson and Sons, 1880), pp. 32, 33.

3. Ibid., p. 34.

4. J. D. Douglas, ed., *The New International Dictionary of the Christian Church* (Grand Rapids: Zondervan Publishing House, 1974), p. 1043.

5. S. Cheetham, *A History of the Christian Church* (London: Macmillan and Co., Ltd., 1907), p. 189.

6. James Nichols, *History of Christianity 1650-1950* (New York: The Ronald Press Co., 1956), p. 74.

7. Shirley Barker, *Builders of New England* (New York: Dodd, Mead and Company, 1965), p. 81.

8. Ryle, *The Christian Leaders of the Last Century*, pp. 37, 40.

9. Ibid., pp. 42, 43.

10. Douglas, ed., *The New International Dictionary*, p. 1044.

TWENTY-ONE GREAT VOICES

⁊ LEWIS SPERRY CHAFER ⁊

Lewis Sperry Chafer's life spanned eight decades, and during his career, he contributed enormously to the area of eschatology by virtue of writing and publishing a dispensational, premillennial eschatology. He experienced and witnessed a vast upheaval in American religion from the 1870s until 1952. But Chafer was no mere spectator to what was occurring religiously; he was deeply involved throughout his life as an evangelist, pastor, author, systematic theology professor and seminary president.

As is true with many gifted individuals, he possessed paradoxical qualities. His father was a graduate of Auburn Theological Seminary, but Chafer, though he was awarded three honorary doctorates, was not a seminary graduate. Nevertheless, his lack of formal theological education did not hinder him, but served as a catalyst to encourage him to study theology intensely. Short in stature and slight of frame, he was fearless of spirit in controversy and debate. He was an ardent evangelist during an era when evangelism was replete with gimmickry and had acquired a reputation of charlatanism. However, Chafer continually spoke against the use of methods in evangelism and in his book, *True Evangelism,* voices his concern over the indiscriminate use of coercion in evangelism.

Chafer retained his membership in the Presbyterian Church, U.S. through he himself was a devoted evangelical who perhaps would have been more comfortable in a more theologically conservative denomination. Born and raised in the Midwest and New England, he was instrumental in establishing a seminary in the heart of the Southwest, Dallas, Texas. Although he was a southern Presbyterian, one of his closest colleagues was an Anglican, W. H. Griffith Thomas. Even though Chafer had no children, it is impossible to calculate how many recognize him as their spiritual father, perhaps even millions revere his teachings.

Born at Rock Creek, Ashtabula County, Ohio, on February 27, 1871, he was the son of the Reverend Thomas Franklin Chafer and Lois Lomira Sperry. Thomas Franklin graduated from Auburn Theological Seminary with the class of 1864 and was the local Congregational minister. Thomas Chafer was born in 1828 and lived until 1882. Thomas Franklin's father, William Chafer, was born in York, England, and came to the United States in 1837. Lewis' mother was born at Rock Creek, Ohio, in 1836 and lived until the fall of 1915. Her father, Asa Sperry, was a licensed Welsh Wesleyan preacher. His maternal grandmother of Irish descent was Ann Sperry.[1]

When Lewis was eleven years old, his father died, leaving a family of three children: one daughter, Maryette, and two sons, Rollin and Lewis. Lewis, the youngest, inherited many of the finer traits of his father. He wrote his sermons with great care; discipline marked his thinking and writing style. C. F. Lincoln claims: "This trait of painstaking study on the part of the father reflected and magnified in the untiring devotion of Doctor Chafer to ceaseless searching of the Scriptures in the severest of inductive study."[2]

The details of Chafer's formative years, however, have not been documented. He attended public school until age twelve, just one year after the death of his father. He assumed his share of the household responsibility by working on a nearby farm. Dr. Edwin C. Deibler, a former student of Chafer and one who traveled for years with Chafer in evangelistic and Bible conference ministries, describes Chafer as "small of stature, but tough.... Had spent years on the farm."[3]

From 1885 to 1888 he attended Lyme Institute of New Lyme, Ohio. Here he discovered a talent which characterized his entire ministry – music. "An old photo shows him in the New Lyme Band, playing the violin, and his sister Maryette playing the triangle." [4] His natural ability in music proved to be of importance in his eighty-one years as an evangelist, pastor, and even seminary professor and president. Chafer was a gifted musician, and he believed the gospel could be presented also through the medium of music, since people are less defensive while listening to music than while listening to an evangelist or minister speak. Also he believed music is edifying to the saints.

His widowed mother moved the family to Oberlin, Ohio, with the intention of providing Lewis an opportunity for education at Oberlin College and Conservatory of Music. Lewis attended this school from 1889-1892, and here his ability in music matured. The years at Oberlin meant more to Chafer than just the acquiring of proficiency in music since he met his future wife, to whom he was married in 1896. They eventually co-authored and published seventeen hymns between 1909-1917, which are contained in their work entitled, *Selected Hymns.*[5]

Edwin C. Deibler states concerning this musical team: "Prior to his [Chafer] days as an evangelist, he was a gospel musician, with his wife Loraine. They served as a musical team; he the choir director, song leader and soloist, she as the accompanist and arranger."[6]

Oberlin College was founded by the revivalist Charles G. Finney. One might suppose that the Arminian theological atmosphere greatly influenced Chafer's theological thought. But Chafer did not enroll in one theology course. Also, his professors of music were not necessarily evangelically or even theologically minded "because the teachers were hired for their musical ability rather than their piety."[7] But Sydney Ahlstrom spoke of Oberlin as a "center of influence for revival theology,"[8] and it cannot be doubted that the influence of the atmosphere of Oberlin had an impact upon the evangelistic thinking and career of Chafer. He spent one year in the preparatory school and two years in the conservatory. In 1892 he graduated from Oberlin Conservatory of Music and ended his formal academic career.

Central to the entire career of Lewis Sperry Chafer was his conversion experience. Dr. John A. Witmer, who personally knew Chafer, believes Chafer was only seven at the occurrence of his conversion and that his conversion experience was the result of responding to an evangelistic message preached by an evangelist named Scott.[9] Howard also suggests this age when he speaks of a religious crisis in Chafer' life at the age of seven. Howard writes:

> At seven he had a definite religious crisis but no one showed any interest in him at the time. "If there had been child evangelism then," he notes, "they would have landed me high and dry, but people weren't interested in children then and I don't know just what happened." [10]

One cannot be definite concerning this "religious crisis" although it does appear Chafer indeed had a a religious experience as a child of seven. Throughout his life, Chafer believed God had directed His grace toward him at the time of his conversion, and the theme of grace became a dominant emphasis in his ministry; thus, he welcomed the title. "Apostle of Grace." Toward the end of his life, Chafer wrote in his culminating work, the *Systematic Theology:*

> Sovereign grace originates and is at once a complete reality in the mind of God when He, before the foundation of the world, elects a a company who are by His limitless power to be presented in glory conformed to the image of His Son. By so much they are TO be to all intelligences the means by which he will manifest the exceeding riches of his grace. (Eph. 2:7). This manifestation will correspond to His infinity and will satisfy Him perfectly as the final, all-comprehensive measurement of His attribute of Grace.[11]

However, grace for Chafer was intimately related to eschatology since he believed the individual's ultimate salvation is derived solely from the grace of God.[12] At the conclusion of his volume on eschatology in the *Systematic Theology*, Chafer writes:

> The location of the third heaven has never been revealed, but it is the home of the Father, the Son, and the Holy Spirit, and has never been inhabited by any created being until the present age. When a believer dies, he goes at once to be with Christ (2 Cor. 5:8; Phil. 1:23) and therefore takes up his abode in that sphere. Thus all believers will be brought into that place of glory at the coming of the Lord, and the third heaven is being populated at the present time. Salvation consists

in fitting individuals for that heavenly sphere.[13]

After his studies at Oberlin were complete, Chafer pursued the career of evangelist for the next seven years. He had been prepared for this profession early in life because of the years he had spent in the parsonage as the son of a minister, his personal conversion experience, and the talents which he developed further at Oberlin College, a school which was very much part of the revivalistic tradition. He became an evangelistic singer until approximately the turn of the century.

Chafer was associated with many well-known evangelists, but he was particularly involved with Arther T. Reed.[14] In 1896 he married Ella Loraine Case. She had been a vital part of his ministry since his studies at Oberlin.

Music was central to his ministry throughout his life but especially during his first seven years as an evangelist when he was forming specific opinions of the use of music in evangelism. Years later in 1918, writing from East Orange, New Jersey, he explains:

> Science has not gone far, and perhaps cannot, in discovering and analyzing the underlying cause of the vital force in music; but the effectiveness of music may easily be traced through its three fundamental elements — rhythm, melody, and harmony...
>
> ...The varying effects produced in the mind by these elements of music constitute the evidence that music is a language of the soul...
>
> ...There must be strong agreement between the words

of a hymn and the effect of the music. Thus truth is often more effective when it is sung than when it is spoken. Certainly the blessing of God had accompanied the singing of the Gospel.[15]

Chafer's ministry as an evangelist spanned twenty-two years, 1892-1914. Until the late 1890s, however, he was not preaching but was convinced his gift in evangelism was music. A crisis occurred in 1897, and this event was a significant factor in his desire to begin a preaching ministry; he contracted tuberculosis.

The theme of eschatology was interwoven in this experience because for the first time in his life, Chafer became aware of his own mortality. Finally, he fully resigned himself to what he perceived as the will of God for the rest of his life. Chafer's entire preaching and teaching ministry was essentially eschatological in nature. Yes, he spoke of the grace of God, power for living, forgiveness, the spirit-filled life and essential doctrines, but all these topics and subjects were controlled by the overarching theme of humanity's mortality, the need for salvation, and the ultimate encounter with the living God.

His episode with tuberculosis marked a turning point in his ministry because he realized his personal limitations and that he must commit himself fully to the ministry of evangelism. Seeking ecclesiastical endorsement, he was ordained into the Congregational ministry at the age of twenty-nine in the First Congregational Church of Buffalo, New York, but since he believed his true gifts were in evangelism, he once again returned to this ministry. [6] There was a great difference now in his ministry — he returned as a preacher of the Word. He was convinced of his call, and from this time until his death in 1952, fervency and conviction characterized his life and efforts. Although at this point in this life, he did not have the awareness he would have in later years concerning expository preaching and teaching, he was committed to proclaiming the World of God; he had heard the call of God and he submitted to that beckoning.

Soon after his commitment to a career of preaching and teaching, Chafer began examining and changing his opinion of evangelism. Chafer continually questioned the popular evangelism of his day. He became skeptical of evangelistic techniques and in his work, *True Evangelism* speaks of "false forces in evangelism." [17] Of particular interest is his view of the true message of the evangelist:

> The New Testament evangelist is given a particular message to proclaim. That message is the "good news" of the Gospel of Grace; it is therefore a distinct body of truth for the age. His evangel is one of "glad tidings," because if offers freedom from the bondage of the law, with attempts at self-fitting for the presence of God, and because it proclaims a perfect salvation by the power of God through faith in Jesus Christ and His redemption on the cross...[18]

Chafer, then, in contrast to many of his contemporary evangelists, believed in a positive and affirmative message. Howard gives added insight into Chafer's thinking concerning evangelism:

> Chafer had ample opportunity to watch the "methods" of the high-powered evangelists of those days. J. Wilbur Chapman was applying his "machinery" to gospel preaching, organizing his meetings to the point of spotted trained personal workers in every fifth row to converge on the audience during the

invitation. He stormed the big cities with 25 evangelists holding simultaneous meetings. For a while Chafer was one of the 25. But soon, he claims, he began to see dangers in the ordinary methods of "getting decisions," counting raised hands and promptly leaving town. There seemed to be no place for the grace of God or the work of the Holy Spirit, and he began to question the use of methods which do not recognize the Spirit's ministry of revealing the Gospel.[19]

Chafer's book, *True Evangelism,* although not published until 1911, was written in 1901. He came to be known as the evangelist "without methods" and stressed "an entire dependence upon the Spirit to do every phase of the work that has been assigned to Him in the purpose of God."[20] He comments further on the use of methods:

> Likewise, an undue emphasis upon methods in modern evangelism is a almost universal. The erroneous impression exists that the evangelistic efforts should be confined to stated times and seasons, and that impression has led to a far more serious one, namely, that God is only occasionally "on the giving hand"; whereas the Scriptural forces in true evangelism depend upon the unchanging promises of God, the constant abiding presence of the Holy Spirit in the Church, and His continual working through members of the body of Christ.[21]

Many years later in 1947, Chafer wrote an article defending the writing of *True Evangelism.* He stated the reason for writing the book as follows: "The purpose in the main being to record the experiences through which the author had passed in evangelism in relation to the methods of the day and to provide a constructive message on the unchanging truth that souls must be enlightened by the Holy Spirit."[22] The book virtually contains no eschatological or dispensational themes. The work was written before his introduction to C. I. Scofield and his personal study of the Scriptures.

It is apparent that Chafer, though very much within the then current evangelistic tradition, had definite and firm convictions concerning evangelism, convictions which placed him at odds with many if not most of his contemporaries. Because of his reservations with methods in evangelism, many accused him of refusing to give an invitation, as was a common practice among the evangelists of that era. Edwin Deibler states: "Relative to the canard that Chafer was not interested in evangelism and refused to give an invitation, I heard Chafer preach a message in the summer of '38 at the First Baptist church in San Diego and give an invitation afterward to which there was a considerable response."[23]

Chafer appeared as a fervent evangelist, polished but unpretentious. One easily obtains the impression that although chafer was comfortable with evangelism, this was not the area in which his gifts could be used to the fullest. He was too methodical, organized, creative, and perhaps not fully spontaneous to limit himself solely to evangelism. One sees a progression in his personal realization that his best gifts lay in Bible teaching and writing. He wrote his work, *True Evangelism,* in order to correct the flagrant abuses in evangelism. The work was indeed a precursor of his intense desire to fashion a biblical philosophy of his personal faith.

The last quarter of the nineteenth century was a period when Bible and prophetic conferences were very popular. Kellogg writing in 1888 speaks of

An impressive visible illustration in the premillennial conference held in the church of the Holy Trinity, New York, in 1878, when the great assembly at its closing meeting, rising to their feet, passed with great enthusiasm the following resolution: That the doctrine of our Lord's premillennial advent instead of paralyzing evangelistic and missionary effort, is one of the mightiest incentives to earnestness in preaching the gospel to every creature till he comes. Nor is this a matter with them of mere words....[24]

D. L. Moody, who was virtually a household name in the United States and Great Britain during the last quarter of the nineteenth century, exerted a powerful influence upon the theological climate at Northfield, both by his personal teachings and the speakers he brought to Northfield. Through the influence of D. L. Moody, premillennialism became the dominant eschatological position at the Northfield conferences. Sandeen writes: "By 1886 the leaders of millenarian movement had practically taken over the Northfield conferences and transformed it into another of their familiar premillennial gatherings." [25] Theologians and clergymen who took part were not only from the United States but also from Canada and Great Britain. Moody selected leading British clergy to lead evangelistic meetings at Northfield. [26] Northfield indeed became an important chapter in Chafer's life.

In 1903, the Chafers moved to East northfield, Massachusetts. Chafer transferred his ministerial membership to the Presbytery of Troy, New York. Lincoln relates the important relationship which commenced at Northfield:

At that time Dr. C. I. Scofield was pastor of the Congregational Church of Northfield, which had been organized by D. L. Moody, and there was cemented between the two men [Scofield and Chafer] a closeness of fellowship ... which lasted until Dr. Scofield's death in 1921. When Dr. Chafer moved to East Northfield he began at once his service as music leader, along with Ira Sankey, D. B. Towner, George Stibbins and others, in the great Moody Summer Bible Conferences. Mrs. Chafer was the official organist for the conferences.[27]

Chafer was affiliated with Northfield from 1903-1909. During those years, the Northfield Bible Conference featured such biblical expositors and theologians as H. W. Webb-Peploe, G. Campbell Morgan, W. Graham Scroggie, and F. B. Meyer of Great Britain; W. H. Griffith Thomas and A. B. Winchester of Canada; and A. T. Pierson, William B. Eerdman, C. I. Scofield, H. A. Ironside, and George E. Guille of the United States. In later years, Chafer acknowledged the influence of these dispensational, premillennial theologians when he wrote: The association and close acquaintance with some of the world's greatest expositors ... placed before me the ideals of expository preaching based on extended knowledge and familiarity with the Scriptures.[28]

D. L. Moody organized Northfield in 1880 with a view to giving the average church member an opportunity for spiritual renewal. Chafer had this to say about the impact of Northfield:

> Not only does the summer Bible conference minister to the hunger of many, but it has been one of the greatest agencies in transforming Christian lives. In these gatherings, more than has ever ben estimated, lives have been dedicated to God, and

LATE CHRISTIANITY: THE FAITH

true spirituality entered into which as resulted in ministries for God which have gone out to the ends of the earth. A book of personal testimonies from Keswick, Northfield of the earlier days, and from the conferences of later days, would disclose how wonderfully God has provided for the present needs of his people through the summer Bible conferences. What an unnumbered company of Christians are thanking God for the vision and spiritual change which they have received at these great Bible study, missionary and Victorious Life gatherings![29]

During these years to Northfield, Howard relates that Chafer owned a farm in the Northfield area, and he spent the winters in evangelistic campaigns, farmed in the spring, and in the summer led the singing at Northfield with such well-known musicians as Ira Sankey.[30] Mrs. W. R. Moody, daughter-in-law of D. L. Moody, states of Chafer: "I always consider the peak of our singing here was reached under Mr. Chafer. I shall never forget 'Master, the Tempest is Raging,' and so many other hymns which they [the audience] never sang so well for anyone else."[31]

From 1906-1909 and for three weeks in the fall of 1910, he was a teacher of music and Bible at the Mount Hermon School for Boys. Mount Hermon was a secondary school affiliated with Northfield which had a basic curriculum along with Bible. Chafer apparently was very approachable as a teacher and his students readily confided in him. His students found him capable, helpful and likable. He was repeatedly asked if he would consider taking a pastorate in the area and allow interested individuals to be taught pastoral subjects under his supervision[32] He did not grant their request, but the suggestion that he teach pastoral subjects became a powerful though

125

somewhat latent force in his life. Years later he was the primary personality in the founding of a theological seminary in Dallas, Texas.

As a man in his mid-thirties, what changes had taken place in his thinking and life? First, he had not limited himself solely to music but was developing as a preacher and Bible teacher; second, he was meeting and influencing an ever-widening circle of friends and acquaintances; third, he was beginning to see himself as a professional teacher; and fourth, he was developing a critical awareness to speak against and correct abuses in religion such as with the writing of *True Evangelism*.

Chafer did not disclose just how early he accepted dispensational premillennialism. It is known that he heard many who held to such a position at Northfield, and at this location he met C. I. Scofield and formed a close relationship with him, which was nurtured through the years. Perhaps all that can be said with certainty is that Chafer was essentially in agreement with dispensationalism by this period in his life, but he lacked the solid scholarship behind that belief. He was personally convinced but had not studied the full range of dispensationalism. Time would eventually eliminate that lack.

By this period in his career, there were no outstanding achievements. There were no accomplishments which would serve as an anticipation of his future. After all, he had no formal theological training and was trained in music. Perhaps at this time in his life, Chafer himself was not aware of the great potential he possessed. One quality which served him well throughout his life was his great ability to organize, and this characteristic was evident even at a very young age. All the ingredients for a career of prominence appeared to be crystallizing, but there was no clear-cut direction in achieving specific goals. He displayed ability in speaking and writing. His first book, *Satan*, was written in 1909 and is a biblical summary of what the Scriptures teach concerning this subject. *True Evangelism* was published in 1911. People apparently were drawn to him as testified to by his closeness with his students at Mount Hermon.

Witmer believes the Northfield years were crucial for the career of Lewis Sperry Chafer; these years marked a certain *rite de passage* in his life. Witmer cites Chafer's intense belief in the great need for expository preaching and the strong desire to start a a school for the training of ministers as the two major results of the Northfield years. Witmer writes:

> In the years that followed as Dr. Chafer itinerated the evangelistic and Bible conference ministry he made a point of quizzing countless pastors concerning areas in which they felt their seminary course of study failed to prepare them. Invariably the response was that they were not taught the English Bible in order to be able to minister its truths. The conviction slowly crystallized that a seminary was needed with a distinctive curriculum that would equip men to be expositors of the Word of God. Through these contacts and experiences God prepared Lewis Sperry Chafer for a quarter-century to be His instrument in founding Dallas Theological Seminary.[33]

A dispensational and premillennial eschatological foundation would eventually characterize this school. These distinctive emphases were formulated by Chafer himself.[34]

Of all the people Chafer met in his itinerating work as an evangelist during the Northfield days, the one who influenced him the most was Dr. C. I. Scofield, the editor of the *Scofield Reference Bible*. Chafer often likened this relationship to that of a father and a son.[35] The exact date cannot be fixed, but an important meeting took place between Scofield and Chafer which changed the entire direction of the latter's life. At the time, Scofield was pastor of the First congregational Church of Dallas, Texas. Scofield had invited Chafer to hold evangelistic meetings. At the conclusion of the meetings, Scofield convinced Chafer that his gifts in evangelism were not as great as his gifts as a Bible teacher. The two prayed together, and Chafer dedicated his life to a lifetime of biblical study. The commitment to the Lord on the part of Chafer was accomplished on a human level by C. I. Scofield, and in a real sense that commitment on Chafer's part represented a transference of the dispensational and premillennial teachings of Scofield to Chafer. Walvoord places this event during the World War I years.[36] Renfer, however, points out that Scofield was pastor of the First Congregational Church of Dallas between the years 1883-1895 and also from 1903-1910. The meeting between the two could not have occurred during the first date since Chafer and Scofield did not actually meet until 1901. All that can be stated with certainty is that the meeting took place before 1910.[37]

This unusual meeting with Scofield dramatically altered the course of Chafer's life since the latter apparently took to heart Scofield's advice. Especially from this period until the end of his life, Chafer became a prolific writer and gifted Bible teacher. Chafer must have been somewhat unsure of his gifts to have taken so seriously Scofield's comments. Granted, he had a great admiration for Scofield, but Chafer was no longer a young man.

LATE CHRISTIANITY: THE FAITH

One sees a gradual awareness on Chafer's part concerning his best gifts and the need to develop them to the fullest. How significant was the impact of Scofield upon Chafer? *The Sunday School Times* editors wrote that Chafer had "become in a real sense the successor to Dr. Scofield... and is among the most eagerly sought Bible teachers in the United States."[38] The direction of his life was determined.

By the early 1920s, Chafer, then in his fifties, looked for rest from his strenuous ministry of Bible conference activities. However, constantly in his thinking was the need for a school to train ministers. Since the Northfield days when he taught boys at the Mount Hermon School,...he remembered his students' pleas that he might himself start a school for the purpose of training ministers. Chafer writes:"The vision of this specific type of seminary was given to me at least fifteen years before definite steps were taken to ground This work."[39]

From 1924-1952 Chafer combined the responsibilities of seminary professor and president. Although enrollment grew steadily, the first years especially were financially difficult.

The seminary continued to prosper under Chafer's leadership, and by the time of his death in 1952, the enrollment was 257. At the founding of the school in 1924, Chafer wished to keep the enrollment small, around One hundred, but he gradually became aware of the need for expansion. In the 2002-2003 academic year, Dallas Theological Seminary was the largest nondenominational seminary in the world, and with its several extensions, the seminary has approximately 2,000 students. Dallas Theological Seminary offers master's and doctor's degrees and is fully accredited with the

Southern Association of Colleges and Schools and the Association of Theological Schools.

Chafer's wife, Ella Loraine, suffered a stroke in 1941 which left her an invalid until her death in 1944. A second heart attack afflicted Chafer in 1945, and a third attack occurred in 1948. In May of 1952, after finishing his spring semester responsibilities at the seminary, he visited various Pennsylvania cities that were on the Harrisburg Circuit of Bible Conferences. In June 1952, he traveled alone to Seattle and there died on August 22 in the home of personal friends, Mr. and Mrs. Robert O. Fleming. Two months later, Walvoord wrote in *The Sunday School Times:*

> In the span of one short life was gathered the amazing career of musician, evangelist, Bible teacher, theologian, writer, editor, educator, man of faith, man of prayer, and man of deep spiritual understanding of the Scriptures. Like John Calvin, with frail body but keen mind and spiritual vision, Lewis Sperry Chafer left an indelible mark upon his generation. The monuments of his labor continue, and we trust will continue.[40]

LATE CHRISTIANITY: THE FAITH
NOTES ON LEWIS SPERRY CHAFER

1. C. F. Lincoln, "Biographical Sketch of the Author," in *Systematic Theology*, by Lewis Sperry Chafer, vol. 8: *Biographical Sketch and Indexes* (Dallas: Dallas Seminary Press, 1948), p. 4.

2. C. F. Lincoln, "Lewis Sperry Chafer," *Bibliotheca Sacra* 109 (October 1952):332.

3. Edwin C. Deibler, Professor Emeritus of Historical Theology, Dallas Theological Seminary, personal letter, 17 January 1984.

4. John F. Walvoord, "Lewis Sperry Chafer," *The Sunday School Times* 94 (11 October 1952):855.

5. Mr. And Mrs. Lewis Sperry Chafer, *Selected Hymns* (New York: Biglow & Martin Co., n.d.).

6. Edwin C. Deibler, personal letter, 17 January 1984.

7. John Bernard, *From Evangelicalism to Progressivism at Oberlin College, 1866-1917* (Columbus: Ohio State University Press, 1969), p. 106.

8. Sydney E. Ahlstrom, *A Religious History of the American People*, 2 vols. (Garden City, New York: Doubleday & Co., Image Books, 1975), 1:558.

9. John A. Witmer, "What Hath God Wrought — Fifty Years of Dallas Theological Seminary," *Bibliotheca Sacra* 130 (October 1973):292.

10. Wally Howard, "Accident Man," *Sunday School Promoter* 6 (June 1944):19.

11. Lewis Sperry Chafer, *Systematic Theology*, vol. 3: *Soteriology* (Dallas: Dallas

Seminary Press, 1948), p. 284.

12. Ibid. p. 7.

13. Lewis Sperry Chafer, *Systematic Theology*, vol. 4: *Ecclesiology-Eschatology* (Dallas: Dallas Seminary Press, 1948), p. 438.

14. Rudolph A. Renfer,"A History of Dallas Theological Seminary" (Ph.D. dissertation, University of Texas, 1959), p. 85.

15. Lewis Sperry Chafer,"Why Music Reaches Souls," *The Sunday School Times* 60 (23 February 1918): 108

16. Witmer,"What Hath God Wrought," p. 293.

17. Lewis Sperry Chafer, *True Evangelism* (n.p., 1919; rev. ed. Grand Rapids: Zondervan Publishing House, 1967). In chapter one, "False Forces in Evangelism" (pp. 3-23), Chafer outlines the three false forces of men, methods and messages.

18. Ibid., p. 21.

19. Howard,"Accident Man," pp. 20, 54.

20. Chafer, *True Evangelism*, p. iii.

21. Ibid, p. 9.

22. Lewis Sperry Chafer, "An Attack Upon a Book," *Bibliotheca Sacra* 104 (April 1947):130.

23. Deibler, personal letter, 17 January 1984.

24. Samuel H. Kellog, "Premillennialism: Its Relations to Doctrine and Practice," *Bibliotheca Sacra* 45 (April 1888):270.

25. Ernest Sandeen, *The Roots of Fundamentalism* (Grand Rapids: Baker Book House, 1978), p. 175.

26. Ibid., p. 176.

27. Lincoln, "Biographical Sketch of the Author," p. 4.

28. Lewis Sperry Chafer, "Twenty Years of Experience," B*ulletin of Dallas Theological Seminary* 29 (July-September 1943).

29. Lewis Sperry Chafer, "Summer Bible Conferences: Their Meaning," *The Sunday School Times* 62 (24 April 1920):235. A substantial history and analysis of the Northfield Bible Conferences is contained in *James F. Findlay, Dwight L. Moody: American Evangelists, 1837-1899* (Grand Rapids: Baker Book House, 1969), pp. 339-355.

30. Howard, "Accident Man," p. 54.

31. Mrs. Howard Taylor, *Empty Racks and How to Fill Them* (Dallas: Evangelical Theological College, n.d.), p. 8.

32. Ibid.

33. Witmer, "What Hath God Wrought," p. 294.

34. Lewis Sperry Chafer, "The Founding of Dallas Theological Seminary," a tape recorded by Dallas Theological Seminary, n.d.

35. Lewis Sperry Chafer, "What I Learned from Dr. Scofield," *The Sunday School Times* 64 (4 March 1922):120.

36. Walvoord, "Lewis Sperry Chafer," p. 868.

37. Renfer, "A History of Dallas Theological Seminary," p. 9.

38. "A True Theological Seminary," *The Sunday School Times* 66 (6 September 1924):525.

39. Chafer, "Twenty Years of Experience."

40. Walvoord, "Lewis Sperry Chafer," p. 870. Cf. "Dr. Lewis Sperry Chafer, 81, Dies in Seattle," *Dallas Morning News*, 23 August 1952, p. 4.

☙ Conclusion ❧

No one can predict what the twenty-first century will hold for Christianity. With certainty, however, the distinction between various theologies and denominations will continue. More than likely, the Christian church will continue its dialogue with other world religions, cults and sects. Global concerns and interpretations of eschatology and salvation will also perhaps be prominent issues within all branches of Christendom.

These twenty-one leading Christians give a greater appreciation of the past. They lay the foundation for an awareness and an understanding of the future.

TWENTY-ONE GREAT VOICES

❧ SELECTED BIBLIOGRAPHY ☙

Ahlstrom, Sydney, E. *A Religious History of the American People.* 2 vols. Garden City, New York: Doubleday & Co., Image Books, 1975.

Artz, Frederick B. *The Mind of the Middle Ages.* New York: Alfred A. Knopf, 1953.

Bainton, Roland. *Studies in the Reformation.* Boston: Beacon Press, 1963.

Barker, Shirley. *Builders of New England.* New York: Dodd, Mead, and Company, 1965.

Borhmer, R. H. *Road to the Reformation.* Philadelphia: Muhlenberg Press, 1946.

Brinton, Henry. *The Context of the Reformation.* London: Hutchinson Educational Ltd., 1968.

Cairns, Earl. *Christianity through the Centuries.* Grand Rapids: Zondervan Publishing House, 1954.

Campbell, George A. *The Crusades.* New York: Robert M. McBride and Company, 1938.

Cantor, Norman F. *Medieval History.* New York: The Macmillan Company, 1963.

Cheetham, S. *A History of the Christian Church.* London: Macmillan and Co., Ltd, 1907.

Cunningham, William, *The Reformers and the Theology of the Reformation.* Edinburgh: T & T Clark, 1886.

Daniel-Rops, Henri. *The Protestant Reformation.* London: J. M. Dent and Sons Ltd., 1961.

Dannenfeldt, Karl H. *The Church of the Renaissance and Reformation.* St. Louis: Concordia Publishing House, 1970.

Douglas, J. D., ed. *The New International Dictionary of the Christian Church.* Grand Rapids: Zondervan Publishing House, 1974.

Ellingsen, Mark. *The Evangelical Movement: Growth, Impact, Controversy, Dialog.* Minneapolis: Augsburg Publishing House, 1988.

Erickson, Millard J. *Christian Theology.* Grand Rapids: Baker Book House, 1986.

Ferguson, Wallace K., and Bruun, Geoffrey. *A Survey of European Civilizations.* Boston: Houghton Mifflin Company, 1969.

Fisher, George P. *The Reformation.* London: Charles Scribner's Sons, 1906.

Foakes-Jackson, F. J. *The History of the Christian Church.* New York: George H. Doran Company, 1927.

Fogarty, Gerald P. *American Catholic Biblical Scholarship:A History from the Early Republic to Vatican II.* San Francisco: Harper & Row Publishers, 1989.

Fosdick, Harry E. *Great Voices of the Reformation.* New York: Random House, 1952.

Fulton, John, ed. *Ten Epochs of Church History.* 10 vols. New York: Charles Scribner's Sons, 1898. Vol. 2: *The Post-Apostolic Age,* by Lucius Waterman.

Goodspeed, Edgar. *A History of Early Christian Literature.* Chicago: University of Chicago Press, 1942.

Hagenback, K. R. *History of the Reformation in Germany and Switzerland Chiefly.* 2 vols. Edinburgh: T & T Clark, 1878.

Harbison, E. Harris. *The Christian Scholar in the Age of Reformation.* New York: Charles Scribner's Sons, 1956.

Hillerbrand, Hans J. *The Reformation.* New York: Harper & Row Publishers, 1964.

Hulme, Edward. *The Protestant Revolution and the Catholic Reformation.* New York: The Century Company, 1915.

Kerr, Hugh T., ed. *Calvin's Institutes:A New Compend.* Louisville, KY:

Westminster/John Knox Press, 1989.

Kulper, B. K. *The Church in History.* Grand Rapids: William B. Eerdmans Publishing Company, 1964.

Lawson, John. *A Theological and Historical Introduction to the Apostolic Fathers.* New York: The Macmillan Company, 1961.

Lightfoot, J. B. *The Apostolic Fathers.* New York: Macmillan and Company, 1889.

Maynard, Theodore. *Saint Ignatius and the Jesuits.* New York: P. J. Kennedy and Sons, 1956.

Moeller, Wilhelm. *History of the Christian Church.* New York: Swan Sonnenschein and Company, 1892.

Moyer, Elgin. *Great Leaders of the Christian Church.* Chicago: Moody Press, 1951.

Nichols, James H. *History of Christianity 1650-1950.* New York: The Ronald Press Company, 1956.

Rainey, Robert. *The Ancient Catholic Church.* New York: Charles Scribner's Sons, 1902.

Ryle, J. M. C. *The Christian Leaders of the Last Century.* London: T. Nelson and Sons, 1880.

Sandeen, Ernest. *The Roots of Fundamentalism.* Grand Rapids: Baker Book House, 1978.

Schaff, Philip. *History of the Christian Church.* 8 vols. Grand Rapids: William B. Eerdmans Publishing Company, 1910.

Schnuerer, Gustav. *Church and Culture in the Middle Ages.* 3 vols. Translated by George J. Undereiner. Patterson, NJ: St. Anthony Guild Press, 1956.

Setton, Kenneth M., ed. *A History of the Crusades* 5 vols. Philadelphia: University of Pennsylvania Press, 1955. Vol. 1: *The First Hundred Years,* edited by Marshall W. Baldwin.

Stevenson, Carl. *Medieval History.* New York: Harper and Brothers, 1935.

Stevenson, William. *The Story of the Reformation.* Richmond: John Knox Press, 1959.

Stumpf, Samuel. *Socrates to Sartre.* New York: McGraw-Hill Company, 1966.

Thompson, James W. and Johnson, Edgar N. *An Introduction to Medieval Europe.* New York: W. W. Norton and Company, Inc. 1937.

Walker, Williston. *A History of the Christian Church.* New York: Charles Scribner's Sons, 1918.

Weber, Timothy. *Living in the Shadow of the Second Coming.* New York: Oxford University Press, 1979.

Wordsworth, Charles. *A Church History to A.D. 325.* London: Gilbert and Rivington, 1881.

ABOUT THE AUTHOR

Jeffrey Jon Richards is a minister and theology professor who lives with his family in North Carolina. He received the Th.M. degree from Dallas Theological Seminary and the Ph.D. in systematic theology from Drew University. He has done postdoctoral work at Oxford (England), Marburg, and Tuebingen (Germany). He has taught on the faculties of several American and European universities and seminaries.

TWENTY-ONE GREAT VOICES